D1447149

EXPLORING OLD QUEBEC

The Casse-Cou Stairs and Rue du Petit-Champlain
(#40 and 41)

Exploring
Old Quebec

Maude Bonenfant

TRANSLATED FROM THE FRENCH BY
Vicki Marcok

Véhicule Press

Published with the generous assistance of the Book
Publishing Industry Development Program of the
Department of Canadian Heritage and the Société de
développement des entreprises culturelles du Québec
(SODEC).

Photographs: Maude Bonenfant
Cover design: J.W. Stewart
Set in Adobe Minion and Gill by Simon Garamond
Printed by Marquis Book Printing Inc.

Special thanks: Bruce Henry & Helen Meredith

LIBRARY AND ARCHIVES CANADA CATALOGUING IN PUBLICATION

Bonenfant, Maude, 1976-
Exploring old Québec / Maude Bonenfant.
Includes index.
ISBN 978-1-55065-226-0
1. Québec (Québec)—Guidebooks. I. Title.

FC2946.18.B66 2007   917.14'471045   C2007-900642-6

Published by Véhicule Press, Montréal, Québec, Canada
www.vehiculepress.com

Distribution in Canada by LitDistCo
orders@litdistco.ca

Distribution in U.S. by Independent Publishers Group
www.ipgbook.com

Printed in Canada on 100% post-consumer recycled paper.

Contents

Statue of Samuel de Champlain (#5)

Introduction

Québec is one of the most visited cities in North America, for good reason—it has a unique charm. A romantic city, it attracts lovers as well as families and tourists interested in history. Famous visitors have included Charles Dickens, Alexis de Tocqueville, Franklin D. Roosevelt, Winston Churchill, Alfred Hitchcock, Richard Nixon, Charles de Gaulle, François Mitterrand, Elizabeth II, and Ronald Reagan. In 1985 UNESCO named Québec a World Heritage Site. It is the only city in either Canada or the United States to have preserved its original walls and fortifications—although the city has been the scene of armed conflict, many historic buildings remain. The history of the city, the province, the country and North America unfolds on every street corner. The history of the Amerindians, French, English, Scottish, Irish, and Americans has been shared for 400 years in Québec.

Samuel de Champlain, who founded the city in 1608, could envision the potential of the site. Its location on the St. Lawrence River made it a natural starting place for exploration of the territory and transport of goods and settlers. Québec quickly became the port of entry for the whole continent. As well, the river provided a strategic advantage: at Québec it narrows, facilitating control of maritime traffic. At Cap Diamant, which from the river's edge appears unscalable, but the good defensive position provided by nature was reinforced to make it almost impregnable. The growth of the city is based on the topography which divides Old Québec into fortified Upper Town, and commercial Lower Town with its easy access to the river. Taking your time to wander through its stories streets will enhance your visit to the Old Capital, and you will be rewarded by many wonderful discoveries.

GENERAL INFORMATION

Centre Infotouriste Québec
(Québec Infotourist Centre)
12 Rue Ste-Anne (facing Place d'Armes)
1.877.BONJOUR (1.877.266.5687)
Open daily 9:00 am to 5:00 pm
(8:30 am to 7:30 pm during summer)

Bureau d'informations touristique du
Vieux-Québec (Tourist Information Bureau)
835 Avenue Wilfrid-Laurier (near military parade ground)
Open daily 9:00 am to 5:00 pm
1.877.266.5687 / 418.641.6290

Québec City Museum Card
For $40 this three-day pass allows entry to 11 of Québec's museums and tourist attractions, two days' unlimited access to city buses, as well as other benefits. You can purchase cards at most museums and historic sites.

Post Office
5 Rue du Fort
1.800.267.1177
Open Monday to Friday 8:00 am to 7:30 pm; Saturday and Sunday 9:30 am to 5:00 pm

Newspapers
The major French-language newspapers in Québec are *Le Soleil* and *Le Journal de Québec*, as well as the Montréal dailies *La Presse* and *Le Devoir*. *The Gazette*, Montréal's English-language daily is also available. The free French-language entertainment weekly *Voir* lists many events and activities, as does the *Quebec Chronicle-Telegraph*, the longest surviving newspaper in North America.

Jean-Lesage International Airport

418.640.2600
Complete information about arrivals and departures, as well as directions to the airport, is available at www.aeroportdeQuébec.com

Gare du Palais (train station)

VIA Rail Canada
450 Rue de la Gare-du-Palais
1.888.842.7245
www.viarail.ca

Gare d'autocars de la Vieille Capitale (bus station)

Autocars Orléans (largest company using station)
320 Rue Abraham-Martin
418.525.3000

Port of Québec

150 Rue Dalhousie
418.648.3640
www.portQuébec.ca

Réseau de transport de la Capitale (RTC) (city busses)

418.627.2511
Day passes are available. Routes, schedules and cost (about $2.50/ticket) available at www.rtcQuébec.ca

Taxis

Coop Taxi
418.525.5191
Coop Taxi offers guided tours of the city.

Bus Tours
Québec Tours
418.836.8687, 1.800.672.5232
www.Québec-tours.com
Dupont Tours
418.649.9226, 1.800.558.7668
www.tourdupont.com
Les tours du Vieux-Québec
418.664.0460, 1.800.267.8687
www.toursvieuxQuébec.com

Parking
Parking is available at numerous places in Old Québec: at City Hall, Château Frontenac, Place D'Youville, the Marie-Guyart Building on the National Assembly grounds, and on the quays of the Old Port across from the Musée de la Civilisation.

HOW TO USE THIS GUIDE

Walking tours
Seven walking tours are presented in this guide. At a comfortable pace all seven can be done in three days (in or out of the order presented). But if you have less time, or if you prefer a more limited amount of walking, here are some suggestions: The main walking tours are numbers 1, 2, and 3 (and 7, which is outside the walls of Old Québec).
Tour 7 is the longest.
The most physically demanding tours are 4, 6, and 7.

If your time is limited
Do tours 1, 2, and 3 and at the end of tour 3 take the funicular up to the Château Frontenac instead of continuing on to tour 4.

If you have more time
Before you begin the tours, visit the Observatoire de la Capitale (#112) for a panoramic view of the whole city.

Thematic itineraries
The final section of the book proposes some thematic itineraries. Just follow the numbers from one location to another.

Plaques and interpretation panels
Check the façades of buildings because there are numerous informative plaques which have not been listed in the book. The city has installed a number of interpretation panels that provide additional information.

Streets
The street signs in Old Québec often include a short description of the origin of the street name.

Rue Sous-le-Cap (#69)

A BRIEF HISTORY OF QUÉBEC CITY

Three or four thousand years ago, what is now Place Royale in Québec's Lower Town was regularly used by Amerindians for fishing and trade.

1534	First voyage by Jacques Cartier and the founding of New France (under King François I). Cartier and his crew wintered over at the Iroquoian village Stadacona; the Amerindian chief was Donnacona.
1608	(July 3) Founding of the city of Québec by Samuel de Champlain (under Henri IV).
1615	Arrival of the first missionaries, the Recollets (Franciscans).
1617	The first colonists, Louis Hébert and his family, settled in Québec's Upper Town.
1625	Arrival of Jesuit missionaries
1629	The Kirke brothers take control of Quebec until driven out by the French in 1632.
1633	The colony returned to French control (under Louis XIII).
1639	Arrival of Augustinian nursing and Ursuline teaching nuns on the *Saint-Joseph*.
1645	The city contained about ten buildings (under Louis XIV).
1659	Monsignor François de Montmorency-Laval, Québec's first Catholic bishop, arrived.
1663	Séminaire du Québec founded.
1663-1673	With the arrival of 770 single women known as "the King's daughters" (*les Filles du Roy*), Quebec's population tripled.
1666	The city had 547 inhabitants.
1681	The population had grown to 1,345 inhabitants.
1688	Construction began on the Church of l'Enfant

	Jésus, which became Notre-Dame-des-Victoires in 1711.
1690	Defeat of an attack on Québec by Admiral Sir William Phips and his British forces and 2,000 Massachusetts militiamen.

1690 and 1693 Construction of the first two fortifications.

1745	Construction of a third fortification (under Louis XV).
1755	The city had approximately 7,000 inhabitants (French North America had between 60,000 and 70,000 inhabitants; the British colonies numbered approximately 1,200,000).
1759	France and England fought in New France (part of the Seven Years' War).
July 13	A French victory at the Battle of Beauport. Siege of Québec: for three months English troops bombarded Québec from Lévis across the St. Lawrence River.
Sept. 13	Battle of the Plains of Abraham, General Wolfe leading the British troops and General Montcalm, the French troops. Defeat of the French forces. Québec passed into English hands (the Conquest).
1760	Battle of Sainte-Foy.
1763	The Treaty of Paris ended the Seven Years' War between France and England; Canada officially became a colony of England.
1765	Founding of the Scottish Presbyterian Congregation.
1774	The Québec Act relaxed British laws for its French-speaking subjects in North America (under George III).
1775	American troops attempted to take possession of Québec.
1791	Implementation of Constitutional Act which divied

Quebec into two provinces—Upper Canada (now Ontario, mostly English-speaking) and Lower Canada (mostly French-speaking). Québec City named capital of Lower Canada.

1793   Jacob Mountain, first Anglican bishop, arrived in Québec.

1820   Construction of the Québec Citadel (under Lord Marlborough).

1831   Québec had about 30,000 inhabitants.

1832   Cholera epidemic.

1837-1838: Patriots Rebellion (or Rebellion of 1837—armed revolt by "Canadiens" against British rule).

1840   Act of Unification reunited Upper and Lower Canada into United Canadas.

1840-1850: Flood of Irish immigrants to Québec.

1847   Typhus epidemic.

1852   Founding of Laval University, the first French-language university in the Americas.

1856   Founding of the Community of Sisters of the Good Shepherd (Soeurs du Bon-Pasteur).

1860-1900: Québec's growth and development slowed, in part because of increases in customs duties.

1867   British North America Act established Canada as a federation of four provinces (Québec, Ontario, Nova Scotia, and New Brunswick).

1871   Withdrawal of British troops (3,000 soldiers).

1918   Spanish flu epidemic.

1919   Official opening of the Québec bridge to the south shore.

1943-1944: Québec Conferences: Winston Churchill, Franklin D. Roosevelt and William Lyon Mackenzie King met to plan D-Day and the rebuilding of Europe.

1954   First Québec Winter Carnival in February.

1960s	The Quiet Revolution profoundly changed Québec and the Québécois; Québec entered the "modern era".
1976	Parti Québécois under René Lévesque won political power with the goal of Québec independence.
1980	First referendum on Québec independence.
1984	Visit of Pope John Paul II.
1985	Old Québec recognized as World Heritage Site by UNESCO.
1987	Québec hosted World Francophone Summit.
1995	Second referendum on Québec independence.
2001	Québec hosted Summit of the Americas.
2002	New city of Québec created by amalgamating surrounding cities and suburbs. The city now has about 480,000 inhabitants.
2008	Québec City's 400th anniversary, and Roman Catholic World Eucharistic Congress.

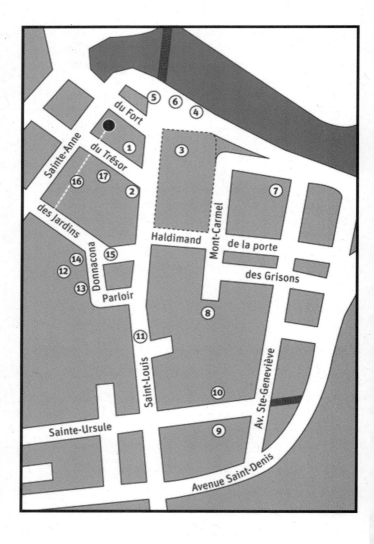

Tour 1

Château Frontenac and Ursuline Monastery

START: PLACE D'ARMES

1. Place d'Armes

Place d'Armes became the official name for this site in 1660; it had previously been called the Place du Fort, the Place du Château, and the Grande Parade. Under the both the French and English regimes it was the military parade ground until the construction of the Citadel in the 19th century. The square became a public park in 1865, and the Monument de la Foi (monument to Faith) was added in 1916. This fountain was erected to commemorate the tricentennial of the arrival in 1615 of four Récollets (Franciscans) the first missionaries in New France. Father Dolbeau and Brother Duplessis built a chapel near l'Abitation (built in 1608), the home of Samuel de Champlain, the "father of New France". Father Caron founded a mission in Huronia and celebrated the first mass there. Father Jamet was the first Superior of the mission in New France, and celebrated the first mass at Sault-au-Récollet in Montreal in 1625, with Champlain in attendance. The monument is 2.7 metres tall and weighs over 1800 kilos. It was cast in a mold from the Catholic Institute in Vaucouleurs in France and symbolizes Christian faith.

2. Gérard-D.-Lévesque Building

The Récollet monastery and chapel once stood here, across from Place d'Armes, at the corner of Rue St-Louis. The missionaries had acquired the land for their buildings, which were destroyed by fire in 1796, from Monsignor de Saint-Vallier, the second bishop of New France. After the Conquest (1759) the land and buildings were confiscated by the British Crown which, in 1800, began construction of a court house (François Baillairgé was the architect) on the site of the monastery. In 1873 the court house burnt down; it was rebuilt between 1883 and 1887 and remained a court house until 1983. It now houses the office of the Québec Finance Ministry, and has been renamed the Gérard-D.-Lévesque Building, honouring the former Québec politician who was in office from 1956 to 1993. The Anglican Cathedral of the Holy Trinity stands on the site of the former Récollet chapel.

3. Château Frontenac

The location of the Château Frontenac, on Dufferin Terrace near the funicular, was the site of Fort Saint-Louis, begun by Champlain in 1620. It was enlarged to become a fortress and then a château and from 1648 until 1834, as Château Saint-Louis, it served as the residence of the colonial governors. (Fort Saint-Louis is currently the site of a dig. See: www.pc.gc.ca/lhn-nhs/qc/saintlouisforts/natcul/ arch1a_e.asp) Beside it, in 1784 construction began on the château of Frederick Haldimand, governor of the colony at the time; he built Château Haldimand as a new residence for future governors. In 1834 the Château Saint-Louis was completely destroyed by fire, and in 1892 the Château Haldimand was razed to make way for the Château Frontenac. You can see a trace of the Château Saint-Louis in the interior courtyard of the Château Frontenac, above the porte-cochère: a Maltese cross carved into the stone and painted red. Charles

The Château Frontenac viewed from the Petit-Champlain
Quarter in the Lower Town (#3)

Huault de Montmagny, who followed Champlain as governor from 1636 to 1648, was a knight of the order of Malta. You enter the interior courtyard through an archway from Rue St-Louis, directly across from Place d'Armes.

The château's name honours Louis de Buade, count of Palluau and Frontenac (1622-1688), the governor of New France from 1672 to 1682 and from 1689 to 1698. He defeated English Admiral Phips' attempt to take Québec. The English left Boston with 32 ships, arrived at Québec on October 16, 1690, and immediately sent an emissary to demand the surrender of the colony. Frontenac tricked the emissary, blindfolding him as he was brought through the city, where he heard what he thought was a large noisy crowd ready to fight. When the emissary arrived at the Château Saint-Louis, Frontenac declared, "I have nothing to say to your general except from the mouths of my canons and guns; this is not how a man of my standing is summoned." Ever since, "from the mouths of my canons" has been an expression of defiance. But Frontenac is also celebrated for bragging that he had shared the favours of Mme de Montespan, one of Louis XIV's mistresses. As well, he requested that, after his death, his heart be sent to his wife in France. However, she had been separated from him for most of their marriage, and refused to accept the gift! She made them send it back.

The indisputable symbol of Québec, the Château Frontenac, is a luxury hotel which was the set for Alfred Hitchcock's movie (starring Montgomery Clift and Anne Baxter) *I Confess* (1953), among many others. Built for the Château Frontenac Company by New York architect Bruce Price, it was bought by Canadian Pacific Railways and opened in 1893. There have been numerous expansions, including the central tower in 1924. Today it is an 18-storey hotel with more than 600 rooms. There are two main restaurants in the Château: Le Champlain under chef Jean Soulard, and the Café de la Terrasse (which is more moderately priced). You can also take tea (with sandwiches and scones) in the afternoon from Monday to Saturday (reservations: 418.266.3905). Guided tours of the Château (with costumed guides making it a somewhat theatrical experience) are available and take about 50 minutes. Information: 418.691.2166

Guided tours: From May 1 to October 15, daily: 10:00 am to 6:00 pm; from October 15 to April 30, Saturday and Sunday only: 1:00 pm to 5:00 pm

Entry fees: Adults $8.50, seniors $7.75, children (6 to 16 years) $6.00

4. Dufferin Terrace

The governor, Lord Durham (1792-1840) began construction of the first terrace on the ruins of the Château Saint-Louis (destroyed by fire in 1834) in 1838. In 1879 the newly enlarged terrace was opened. The terrace is named after Lord Dufferin (1826-1902), who was Governor General of Canada between 1872 and 1878. He saved the fortification from destruction planned by city authorities. Every winter since 1894 there has been a wonderful ice slide on the terrace. The Promenade des Gouverneurs (Governors' Walk) (#120) is at the south-western end of the terrace, then climbs the stairs that circle the Québec Citadel (#101) to arrive at the Parc des Champs-de-Battaille (National Battlefields Park) (#118).

There is a fine view of Lower Town near the guardrail because you are at the top of the cliff of "le cap", which Champlain often called "the mountain". Across the river is Lévis, from where the British bombarded Québec in 1759. Downstream (to your left) is Île d'Orléans, the bridge to the island, and the Charlevoix mountains. The river is the "high-way of the country" because it has been the main trans-portation, communication, and commercial artery since the beginning of the colony. It has always had a crucial role in any development plans for eastern North America. Today more than 3,000 ships annually use it to sail between the Atlantic and the Great Lakes.

5. Statue of Samuel de Champlain

The large statue at the corner of the Château (near the funicular) is of Samuel de Champlain, considered the Father of New France. He was born in 1570 in Brouage, near La Rochelle, France, and was an explorer and geographer. He convinced Henri IV to establish a colony in New France, and crossed the Atlantic a second time, entering the valley of the St. Lawrence river valley. On July 3, 1608 he founded Québec, taking the name of the promontory from the Amerindian term for "where the river narrows" or "debark". He wanted to establish a permanent fur trading post, and built l'Abitation de Québec (the Québec Habitation). It consisted of three two-storey buildings that were partially built in France, in a U-shaped formation surrounding a small enclosed courtyard. L'Abitation was protected by earthwork ramparts and a ditch with a drawbridge permitting access. Initially there were 28 men, but the winter's scurvy killed 16 of them. Jean Duval, one of the men, wanted to kill Champlain and sell the settlement to the Spanish, but he was captured and executed. Terrence Malick's film *The New World* (2005) gives an idea of what the atmosphere was like in such a place. If the tension was not enough, there was the war with the Amerindians which pushed Champlain into an alliance with the Hurons and Algonquins against the Iroquois who were allies of the English. In 1619 he was named Lieutenant Governor of Québec, and in 1623 the settlement's first stone buildings were constructed. Champlain died on December 25, 1635 in Fort Saint-Louis. His coffin was placed in the chapel of Notre-Dame-de-la-Recouvrance (#25), but numerous excavations have not found the exact location.

The statue erected in his honour was the work of Paul Chevré, a Parisian sculptor, and was completed between 1896 and 1898. The statue and base measure 14 metres tall, but the statue itself is 4.5 metres tall. The base is stone from Château-Landon, the same as used for l'Arc de Triomphe and the basilica of Sacré-Coeur de Montmartre in Paris. Unfortunately this stone does not resist cold temperatures well, and restoration work had to be done in 2006 and 2007. The angel on the base symbolizes the proclamation of glory of the Father of New France. There is no authenticated portrait of Champlain, so there is some question about how accurate his image is. In fact, it is more probably a likeness of Michel Particelly d'Emery (1596-1650), controller of finance under Louis XIV who was accused of fraud.

Not far from the statue is a monument commemorating the naming of Québec as a World Heritage Site by UNESCO (United Nations Educational, Scientific and Cultural Organization) in 1985.

6. Funicular

From Dufferin Terrace, near the statue of Samuel de Champlain, a funicular (vertical cable-car) connects Upper and Lower Town. It is the only one of its kind in Canada, rising 60 metres over a distance of 64 metres, at a 45 degree angle. The first steam-driven funicular was built by William Griffith in 1879 and was used only in the summer months. Alexander Cummings electrified it in 1907. In 1945 it was completely destroyed by fire but was rebuilt with metal-clad cabins in 1946. In 1998 it was completely refitted and modernized. To descend to Lower Town, the entrance to the funicular is on Dufferin Terrace beside the Château Frontenac. When taking the trip down, look to your right under the Dufferin Terrace to see one of the guard posts of old Fort Saint-Louis. The trip to Upper Town leaves from

the Maison Louis-Jolliet (#43) in the Petit-Champlain section
of Lower Town.

Information: 418.692.1132

Opening hours: Daily 7:30 am to 11:30 pm

Fee: $1.50 per person

7. Jardin des Gouverneurs (Governors' Gardens)

Walk towards the opposite end of the Dufferin Terrace. You
will pass a park bordering the Château Frontenac above the
Terrace (you can use the stairs). This garden, laid out in 1647,
appeared on city plans by 1660, making it the oldest official
garden in North America. It is located just inside the first
palisade built in 1690 on the far side of Avenue Sainte-
Geneviève. Surrounded by low walls, until 1838 it was
reserved for the use of governors, but is now open to the
public.

The garden contains an obelisk in homage to Louis
Joseph de Saint-Véran, Marquis de Montcalm (1712-1759),
the commanding general of the French army, and James
Wolfe, commander of the English army, who fought the Battle
of 1759 and died on September 13 and 14, respectively. The
inscription, by Dr. John Carlton Fisher, is in Latin and means
"Their courage gave them the same fate; history the same
fame; and posterity the same monument." This is the oldest
commemorative monument in Québec. It was erected in 1827
at the initiative of Lord Dalhousie, the Governor of Canada,
and was the first indication of any *rapprochement* between
Francophones and Anglophones in Québec following the
British Conquest of 1759.

8. Parc Cavalier-du-Moulin

The United States Consulate is just past the small park at the
corner of Rue des Carrières and Avenue Sainte-Geneviève—
a terra cotta brick building constructed in 1935. Walk along

Rue Mont-Carmel, beside the Château Frontenac and the Parc des Gouverneurs and cross Rue Haldimand into the park. Parc Cavalier-du-Moulin is on a hillock that has been officially called Mont Carmel since 1640. In 1663 Simon Denis de la Trinité built a stone windmill on this site. During the 1690s French troops erected a high wall around the mill and installed three canons. The military construction—called a *cavalier*—overhung the surroundings and was used as a redoubt during the 1759 siege of Québec.

Go back along Mont Carmel and turn right on Rue des Grisons—named in 1689 after the graybeards, *les grisons*, going to and from the mill on Mont Carmel. At Rue St-Denis turn right: the park across the street, as well as the fortifications, are a part of the Citadel of Québec (#101). Follow St-Denis to the stairway on your right, at the bottom of the stairs is Rue Ste-Ursule. Walk along Ste-Ursule to the two churches.

9. Chalmers-Wesley United Church - Église Unie Saint-Pierre

The larger church on your right is both Chalmers-Wesley United Church and Église Unie Saint-Pierre. Under the French Regime French Protestants were forbidden from living in New France or practicing their faith there. After the English Conquest (1759), they took advantage of their new religious freedom and founded Saint Jean, a French Presbyterian parish. English Protestants who arrived with the Conquest founded Chalmers-Wesley, but religious services with a minister did not begin until 1800. The congregation met in a rented house until 1816 when they moved to Saint Jean, their first church, on Rue Ferland. In 1853 the congregation moved to Chalmers Church (named after a Scottish theologian). After many Methodist, Presbyterian, and Congregational Churches joined together as the United Church of Canada in 1925, Wesley Methodist and Chalmers Presbyterian became Chalmers-Wesley United in 1931. Since 1987 the church has been home to both Chalmers-Wesley and the French-speaking parish of Saint Pierre. The building was constructed in 1853, and the rich stained-glass windows were created by W. J. Fischer between 1905 and 1913. The interior is renowned for its exceptional acoustics, and its musical and choral tradition is an important aspect of the church. There are concerts open to the public every Sunday at 6:00 pm during the summer.

Information: 1.417.692.3422

10. Notre-Dame du Sacré-Coeur Sanctuary.

Facing Chalmers-Wesley United Church is the Catholic Notre-Dame du Sacré-Coeur Sanctuary. Designed by the architect François-Xavier Berlinguet (1836-1916), it was built to honour the Virgin Mary by the Missionnaires du Sacré-Coeur in 1909 and 1910. The stained glass was created by Henri Perdriaux. The chapel is a replica of the Notre-Dame du Sacré-Coeur Chapel in Issoudun, France, where devotion to Our Lady of the Sacred Heart originated and where the Missionnaires du Sacré-Coeur, who maintain the sanctuary, were founded. In 1902 the Missionnaires moved into the building on Rue Ste-Ursule.

Hours: 7:00 am to 8:00 pm
Fee: Free

11. Rue St-Louis

Continue along Rue Ste-Ursule to Rue St-Louis and turn right. The name refers to Fort Saint-Louis (#3) that most probably honours King Louis XIII of France (1601-1643). The street, laid out in 1630, was straightened during the English regime in the nineteenth century. At the corner of Rue Corps-de-Garde look for the cannonball embedded in the roots of a tree. It is said that this cannonball dates from the 1759 war (it is an English cannonball—only the English used 32-pound cannonballs). No one knows who placed the cannonball here. In the background you see the Parc du Cavalier-du-Moulin near the stone wall, and the building just to your right is where General Montcalm died (the Ursulines kept his skull as a relic for a long time).

At the corner of Rue des Jardins (it has had this name since the seventeenth century), and across the street, is the restaurant Aux Anciens Canadiens, named after the novel *Les Anciens Canadiens* (1863) by Philippe-Joseph Aubert de Gaspé (1786-1871), a well-loved author who lived in this house from 1815 to 1824. The house was built in 1674 for the master roofer François Jacquet dit Langevin, and is possibly the oldest house in Old Québec.

The Consulate of France is at 25 Rue St-Louis at the corner of Haldimand. The Capitulation of Québec was signed in this house on September 18, 1759; and the Duke of Kent lived here from 1791 to 1794.

12. Monastère des Ursulines (Ursuline Monastery)

Walk back to Rue du Parloir and turn right. The Ursuline Monastery is in front of you on Rue Donnacona (named for the Amerindian chief of Stadacona who was captured by Jacques Cartier in 1536 and exiled to France, never to return). The Compagnie de Ste-Ursule, founded in 1535 in Italy, became a religious order in Paris in 1612. It was established in Québec in 1639 by Marie Guyart, who was born in France in 1599, married, and had a son. After the death of her son she entered the Ursuline order in 1631 and became Marie de l'Incarnation in 1633. She arrived in Québec in 1639 to found, with two other Ursulines and Madame de la Peltrie, the first Ursuline monastery and the first school for girls in North America. As Mother Superior, she worked with French-speaking girls as well as with Amerindian girls, learning four aboriginal languages to facilitate communication with the Amerindians. For 33 years she worked for the good of the colony and is referred to as the "Mother of New France". She died in 1672 and was beatified in 1980 by Pope John Paul II.

The first wing of the monastery, the Saint-Augustine wing, was built in 1642; a dozen additional wings were added through the centuries. Eight other additions complete the monastery of today, still occupied by the religious community, but closed to visitors. Only the chapel adjoining the Marie de l'Incarnation Centre is open to the public from May to October. It is possible to visit the tomb of Marie de l'Incarnation.

Information: 418.694.0413

Hours: Tuesday to Saturday from 10:00 am to 11:30 am and from 1:30 pm to 4:30 pm, and Sunday from 1:30 pm to 4:30 pm (closed in December and January)

Fee: Free

An amusing anecdote: After the Conquest, the Highlanders, Scottish soldiers who fought beside the English forces, provided the Ursulines with wood during the winter of 1759-1760. The Ursulines considered the Scottish clothing (kilts) inappropriate for Québec's frigid climate, and it must be said, for their chaste eyes. They decided to knit them longer stockings in the traditional red and white plaid, keeping the soldiers warm and the nuns comfortable. Some gossips maintained that the nuns even knitted underwear for the soldiers ...

13. Monument of Marie de l'Incarnation

Directly in front of you facing Rue du Parloir is the statue of Marie de l'Incarnation by Émile Brunet (1942). It was erected to commemorate the tricentenary of the establishment of the Ursuline monastery, and is dedicated to Marie de l'Incarnation, one of the founders of the Catholic church in Canada.

14. Musée des Ursulines et Centre Marie-de-l'Incarnation (Ursuline Museum and Marie de l'Incarnation Centre)

A bit further along Rue Donnacona is the Chapel at the Marie de l'Incarnation Centre (where there is an exhibit about this extraordinary woman), and the Ursuline Museum. The museum is located on the foundations of Madame de la Peltrie's house. A lay benefactress who arrived in New France with Marie de l'Incarnation, Madame de la Peltrie built her house beside the Ursuline Monastery. In 1650 and 1686 the nuns and their students took refuge in her home when the monastery was struck by fire. The house was then destroyed and today the museum is located in a building constructed in 1836. The museum was opened in 1979 and contains an exhibit illustrating the religious life and teaching vocation of the Ursulines. You can view Madame de la Peltrie's furnishings, as well as many objects which evoke the lives of the nuns, as well as everyday life among the French and Amerindians and the cultural exchanges between the Ursulines and the Amerindians. Guided tours are available.

Information: 418.694.0694

Hours: Tuesday to Saturday from 10:00 am to 5:00 pm and Sunday from 1:00 pm to 5:00 pm (from May to September) Tuesday to Sunday from 1:00 pm to 5:00 pm (October to April)

Fee: Adult: $6.00, seniors $5.00, students $4.00, children Free

15. Monument to the Women Teachers of Québec

On the small platform just in front of you at the junction of Des Jardins, Du Parloir and Donnacona streets is the monument to the Women Teachers of Québec, on Tourangelles Square. Unveiled in 1997, it pays homage to all of the women, religious and lay, who have devoted their lives to education in Québec. The hand and quill symbolize the transfer of knowledge and the dedication of the women. It is the work of Jules Lasalle. When close to the statue look to your left to the house at number 6 Rue Donnacona, which appears to be wedged in between the two neighbouring houses. It was built in 1847, and it is said to be the narrowest stone façade house in North America.

16. Artisans by the Cathedral (on the Esplanade beside Holy Trinity Cathedral)

Take Rue Des Jardins and just before Ste-Anne turn right onto the church grounds. Beside the church along Ste-Anne you will find around fifteen kiosks of the Artisans de la Cathédrale. All of the crafts for sale are hand-made in Québec—lovely little treasures of jewelry, ceramics, hats, wooden boxes, blown glass, stained glass, and clothing.
Hours: Open daily from 10:00 am to 10:00 pm from June to the beginning of September.

17. Anglican Cathedral of the Holy Trinity

After the Conquest the English practiced their faith in the Récollet chapel, but after a major fire there in 1796 they moved to the Jesuit chapel beside the college (#76). In 1793 Bishop Jacob Mountain (1749-1825), the founder of the Anglican Church of Upper and Lower Canada, disembarked at Québec. Shortly after his arrival he petitioned King George III for permission to build a cathedral for his diocese, which he received in 1799. The cathedral is based on the design of St. Martin-in-the-Fields in London, with some modifications including the pitch of the roof to avoid snow accumulation. The construction costs were paid by the English Crown. The cathedral was consecrated in 1804, making it the first Anglican cathedral outside of the British Isles.

The church steeple, built in 1830 by Captain William Hall and Major William Robe, is 47 metres tall and houses eight bells—the largest is 842 kilos—which are rung manually and are still used today. This is the oldest carillon in Canada.

Inside the cathedral there are many elements that affirm the cathedral's attachment to English traditions, including George III's coat of arms. Individual pews had doors to hold in heat during winter months (quite unique). The oak used in the building came from Windsor Forest. The stained glass near the altar was created by Clutterbuck and Co. in England and shipped to Québec in molasses barrels to protect it during the voyage. In 1864 the stained glass was dedicated to the memory of the third bishop of Québec, Dr. George Jehoshaphat Mountain (grandson of the first bishop). The Episcopal and royal thrones were crafted from the wood of the old elm tree that had stood beside the Récollet chapel (on the site of the cathedral). It is said the Récollets preached to the Amerindians under that elm tree.

The church crypt contains the remains of Bishop Jacob Mountain and Charles Lennox (1764 -1819), and the fourth Duke of Richmond and Lennox, Governor General of British North America, among others.

Information: 418.692.2193

Hours: Daily from mid-May to mid-October

Fee: Free, guided tours available

Tour ends at Place d'Armes

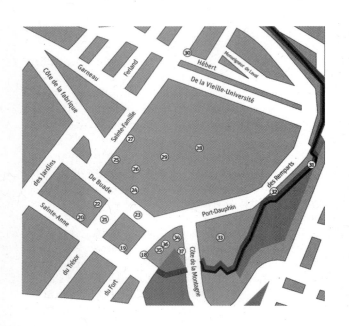

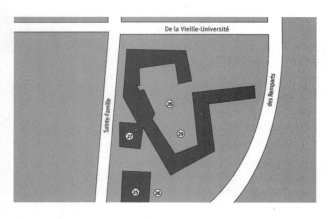

Tour 2

The Québec Seminary and the Basilica-Cathedral

START: PLACE D'ARMES

18. Musée du Fort (Museum of the Fort)

The Musée du Fort is located beside Place d'Armes at the corner of du Fort and Ste-Ursule streets. It was founded in 1964 by Tony Price of the well-known Price family (#75); it is an unusual museum, offering a "diorama" (a half hour long) of the history of the city of Québec. A 40 metre square (430 square foot) model of the city in 1750 is used to present the six sieges of Québec, including the Battle of the Plains of Abraham (#118). The visual and sound effects make for an unusual and graphic way to discover the military and civil history of the city.

Information: 418.692.2175

Hours: February 1 to March 31: Thursday to Sunday 11:00 am to 4:00 pm. April 1 to October 31: 10:00 am to 5:00 pm. November 1 to Christmas: 11:00 am to 4:00 pm

Fee: Adults $8.00, seniors $6.00, students $5.00

19. Centre Infotouriste (Infotourist Centre)

Near the Musée du Fort across Rue du Fort (12 Rue Ste-Anne facing Place d'Armes) is the Infotourist Centre, which is administered by the Ministry of Tourism of Québec. The building dates from 1803, and was the Union Hotel. It has had various occupants, but now it is an information centre for Québec and the surrounding region. You can find information about activities, lodging, restaurants, car rentals, city tours, and more. There are also good city and regional maps, and washrooms.

Information: 1.877.266.5687

Hours: Daily 9:00 am to 5:00 pm (during the summer season 8:30 am to 7:30 pm)

20. Musée de cire de Québec (Québec Wax Museum)

Continue along Ste-Anne to Rue du Tresor. Right at the corner is the Coin du Trésor boutique and what used to be Québec's Wax Museum (22 rue Sainte-Anne). Just as this guide was going to press the museum closed permanently and was replaced by a restaurant. Many of the finer life-size likenesses of famous people went to the Museum of Civilization. The building is a seventeenth century house that was the home of Pierre-Olivier Chauveau (1820-1890), the premier of Québec from 1867 to 1873—the first Québec government after Canadian Confederation.

21. Rue du Trésor

Wander along the open-air gallery of narrow Rue du Tresor, its name unchanged since 1689. Its history even precedes this date. Historian Yves Tessier says that it was originally the office of the Treasury of the Navy of New France. The street is famous, bringing together artists (painters and photographers, mostly) who have been selling their art outdoors, rain or shine, since 1950. Students in fine arts began the tradition of street selling, which the city finally legalized in 1984.

22. Promenades du Vieux-Québec

Just to your left on du Tresor is the entryway to a modest

shopping concours—interior esplanades with boutiques and offices (including the Wallonie-Brussels Delegation) along the length. There is a second entrance off De Buade near the Basilica-Cathedral.

23. Rue De Buade
Return to Rue du Trésor and walk down towards Rue De Buade, named for Louis de Buade, Count of Palluau and Frontenac (#3), Governor of New France. (The Château Frontenac is named after him). The street has existed since his time.

24. Monument to Monsignor Laval
Cross Rue de Buade and look at the bas-relief on the left wall of the basilica, the bronze figures encased in stone. It was created by Jules Lasalle in the 1990s and placed on the outside wall of the chapel dedicated to Monsignor François de Montmorency-Laval (see below) and at the site of his tomb. The work symbolizes the family, one of Laval's cherished values. One side represents a French-Canadian family and the other an Amerindian family. The glass band, visible from the inside, symbolizes the spiritual and religious life of the bishop. The river, the principal means of travel, represents transportation and proselytizing, which was an integral part of New France's mission.

Beside the sculpture, to the right, is the presbytery of Notre-Dame de Québec (on De Buade at the corner of du Fort), previously the episcopal palace. It has been at this location since 1662.

25. Basilique-Cathédrale Notre-Dame de Québec
Continue along Rue de Buade towards Rue Ste-Famille (on your right) to the Notre-Dame de Québec Basilica-Cathedral. In 1633 Samuel de Champlain built Notre-Dame de la

Recouvrance chapel, near the site of the present-day cathedral, but it was destroyed by fire in 1640 (there is a commemorative plaque at 15 Rue de Buade). Notre-Dame de la Paix Church was built in 1647 on the actual site of the cathedral, making it the first Catholic parish and cathedral in New France. In 1650 the first mass was celebrated, and Bishop Laval consecrated the church in 1666. During the Siege of Québec in 1759 the cathedral was destroyed; it was rebuilt in 1766 by architect Jean Baillairgé (1726-1805) using plans by the royal engineer Gaspard Chaussegros de Léry (1682-1756). In 1874 Rome granted it the status of minor basilica ("Royal House"—a designation for a church which has importance in the community and which is also architecturally interesting). There was another major fire in 1922, caused by arson. Once again, the church was rebuilt on the site using the original plans, and in 1925 the new cathedral was inaugurated. It has been designated as an historic monument since 1966.

Inside is the funeral chapel of the first bishop of Québec, François de Montmorency-Laval, whose body was interred there in 1966 beneath a recumbent bronze statue of medieval inspiration by Jules Lasalle. The floor is a black granite map representing the bishop's diocese which stretched from Labrador to the Gulf of Mexico. More than 900 people were buried in the cathedral's crypt between 1654 and 1898, including governors of New France—Frontenac, Vaudreuil, Callières, and Jonquière— and most of Québec's bishops. The glorious high altar built in 1797 is based on the high altar of St. Peter's in Rome, and was sculpted and gilded using the plans of François Baillairgé, who also created the superb baldaquin (canopy) over the high altar between 1787 and 1795. The baldaquin rests on caryatides, and served as a model for many of Québec's churches. Also worth noting is the sanctuary lamp (1663) suspended to the right—a gift from

King Louis XIV to Monsignor de Laval. The lamp is the oldest part of the cathedral, having been saved from numerous fires. The Louis XV pulpit (1776-1784) and the steeple (1766-1805) were created by Jean Baillargé.

The cathedral presents a sound and light show called "Feux Sacrés" (Sacred Fires) May-October. (Call 418.694.0665 for schedule). Group reservations only. Adults $7.50; seniors, students and children over six $5.00.

Hours: Daily from 7:30am to 4:30pm

Fee: Free admission to basilica and guided tours.

26. Centre d'animation François-de-Laval (François de Laval Interpretation Centre)

The Centre, inside the Notre-Dame de Québec Basilica-Cathedral, has various activities documenting the life of Monsignor de Laval, first bishop of New France.

Information: 418.692.0228

Hours: Tuesday to Saturday 10:00 am to 11:30 am and 2:00 pm to 4:30 pm, Sunday 2:00 pm to 4:30 pm

Fee: Free

27. Musée de l'Amérique française (Museum of French America)

Situated on the Séminaire de Québec historic site, the entrance to the Musée de l'Amérique française is visible from the corner of Ste-Famille and Côte de la Fabrique. This former warehouse (1737) became Baillairgé House in 1838. Today it is part of the museum which has its exhibition hall in the interior courtyard of the Séminaire du Québec. Temporary exhibits as well as three permanent exhibits on the history of the French colony of Québec and the development of the educational mission of the Séminaire de Québec are housed in the museum. You can also see the Séminaire collection of (mostly) religious and scientific objects acquired through the centuries. In 1806 it exhibited its first collection—an educational display of scientific instruments. For Québec's 400th anniversary in 2008, France is funding the new Centre de la Francophonie des Amériques—an information centre about the French in the Americas.

You can also take a pleasant and instructive hour-long guided tour of the Séminaire de Québec, mostly along the corridors of the institution. The attractive chapel was built between 1888 and 1890 by Joseph-Ferdinand Peachy (1830-1903), replacing the 1751 chapel which was completely destroyed by fire. The chapel was used for worship until 1990 when the museum took it over. It was deconsecrated in 1995 and converted into a reception hall. Today it is the François-Ranvoyzé Pavilion, named for one of the colony's greatest silversmiths (1739-1819). Don't miss the amazing trompe-l'oeil painting in the chapel. As well, the ceiling which appears to be plaster, and the columns, marble, are covered with painted metal (executed by the Pedlar Metal Roofing Company of Oshawa, Ontario). Who knew? The advantage of the metal ceiling is not only financial (it is much less expensive than plaster), but it is also a less of a fire hazard.

You are now in the entrance of the Musée de l'Amérique française, a perfect starting point to visit the Séminaire du Québec.

Information: 418.692.2843, 1.866.710.8031

Hours: June 24 to Sept. 4: daily 9:30 am to 5:00 pm. Sept. 5 to June 23: Tuesday to Sunday 10:00 am to 5:00 pm

Guided tours: Saturdays and Sundays 1:30 pm and 3:15 pm. Register at the reception desk.

Fee: Adults $5.00, seniors $4.00, students $3.00, children free

28. Séminaire de Québec

Founded in 1663 by Monsignor Laval, the Québec Seminary is the second-oldest educational institution in North America.

(Only Harvard, founded in 1636, is older.) It is the oldest school for boys in Canada. The Séminaire played an essential role in the creation and development of the educational system in Québec, including North America's first Catholic French-language university, Laval, which opened in 1852. The Séminaire's original missions were the training of priests, converting Amerindians, and administering the parishes of the colony. In 1668 Monsignor Laval founded the Petit Séminaire, a boarding school for boys who might enter the priesthood. After the Conquest, courses taught by the Jesuits at the college were cancelled. (The Jesuit order was banned from Québec by the English regime.) The Petit Séminaire took over the responsibility and still teaches students at the secondary level (ages 12 to 17), and since 1987 it has been administered by a lay corporation. The Séminaire de Québec is administered by a religious corporation of diocesan priests (approximately 30 secular priests and 20 seminarians) called the Messieurs du Séminaire de Québec. Laval University's School of Architecture has been located in the Séminaire's buildings since 1988, even though the university moved all of the other faculties to its present location in Sainte-Foy (a suburb) in 1960.

29. Interior Courtyard of the Séminaire de Québec

Even if you are not taking a guided tour, walk into the interior courtyard of the Séminaire, passing the entrance to the Musée de l'Amérique française on your right. For 340 years this courtyard has been the playground for the older students (12 to 17 years old). The building directly in front of you with the sun dial is the oldest of the Séminaire's buildings (1681, the procurator's wing), and which today houses Laval's School of Architecture. Check the hook above the last window on the right side of the building: it was used to haul the trunks and cases of the boarding students up to their dormitory rooms. The top floor was reserved for the dormitories—it was stifling hot in summer, and freezing cold in winter. This floor was also used to hold prisoners taken during the December 31, 1775 attack on the city by American troops led by Benedict Arnold and Richard Montgomery. To the right of the procurator's wing is the parlor wing, and as you walk across the courtyard you pass over the old kitchen, no longer used. The fact that the Séminaire is located on a steep slope explains the anomaly of the kitchen windows opening inwards rather than outwards.

30. Maison Touchet
Return to the entrance to the Musée de l'Amérique française and turn right on Ste-Famille, walk down the hill. At the corner of Ste-Famille and Hébert streets, facing you on your right (at #15) is a low house with an enormous chimney (facing Hébert), five dormers with leaded glass windows and a charming red roof. This is a fine example of the architecture of the French Regime, built for master cooper Simon Touchet between 1747 and 1768.

Turn right on Hébert and look at the attractive old houses on the street. Walk to the end of the street, turn right on Rue des Remparts and cross the street to the low wall. You can look out over part of the Old Port, the Louise Basin, and the market (#67).

31. Les remparts
Rue des Remparts is named for the ramparts, the wall that encircles part of the city. The ramparts were completed in 1811, but in 1878 the height of the walls was reduced by three metres (10 feet) to open up the view for passersby. The canon emplacements were removed as well. During the nineteenth century there was a great deal of prestige in living on this street.

As you climb the hill on des Remparts, the Séminaire de Québec is across the street—more precisely, the Petit Séminaire's lovely building. The parking lot you pass was originally the playground for the oldest students.

32. The Cannons

You will have noticed the many cannons that are almost everywhere in Old Québec. In fact, at the time of the Conquest, there were 180 of them. The French had 4, 8, 12, 16 and 24 pound pieces (the numbers refer to the weight of the cannonballs), with ranges between 2700 and 4000 metres. The British had 2000 cannons on 43 ships and a battery of 21 (32 pound) cannons at Lévis across the river which were used to bombard the city for weeks. At that time cannons were smooth-bore cast iron, charged from the mouth. The bore was cleaned out (to prevent left-over powder from igniting) with a swab, the packing and powder charge were rammed into the breech, the metal cannonball inserted, packing added again, and the powder ignited with a slow match or fuse.

Today there are 183 artillery pieces in Québec including 50 carronades (named for the city of Carron in Scotland)—short, stocky maritime guns mounted on gun carriages of cast iron. There are 78 enormous 18 and 24 pound cannons on carriages with swivel mounts, which are visible from Rue des Remparts.

Between 1840 and 1850 two French captains, Treuille de Beaulieu and Tamisier, developed a rifled cannon barrel with a rear-loading moveable breech. Due in part to these developments, along with important improvements in gunpowder, the effective range of cannons increased, and explosives-filled shells rather than round cannonballs could be fired. Accuracy and effectiveness soared, and Québec's fortifications, the "Gibraltar of America", ceased to be effective because the walls could be pierced by shells. The cannons became museum pieces which we can still admire today.

33. Parc Montmorency

Continue along des Remparts and its name will change to Rue Port-Dauphin. Stop at Montmorency Park on your left. The park is on the site of the first episcopal palace in Québec, erected between 1689 and 1693 by Monsignor de Saint-Vallier (1653-1727), Monsignor Laval's successor. Until 1713 the old episcopal palace was used by religious orders until it became the House of Assembly of Lower Canada in 1791, and then the House of Assembly of the United Canadas until 1840. The building was enlarged in 1831, but a fire in 1854 entirely destroyed it and a new building was built in 1859 and 1860. It was in this building that sessions of the Québec Conference were held in 1864, a precursor to Canadian Confederation in 1867. There is a plaque commemorating this event in the park and a statue of one of Canada's most prominent Fathers of Confederation, George-Étienne Cartier (by George W. Hill, unveiled in1920). In 1883 the building once again burned down, and the City of Québec created a park. In 1904 it was named the Jardin Montmorency to honour both the first bishop of the colony, Monsignor François de Montmorency-Laval and Henri II, duc de Montmorency, viceroy of New France from 1619 to 1625.

A monument to Louis Hébert is at one end of the park. In 1617 he and his wife Marie Rollet and their children arrived at Québec and became its first settlers. Hébert (1575-1627) left Paris, where he had been an apothecary, to come to Québec. He was the first farmer in the colony to live off his land, according to Champlain. The bronze monument is the work of Alfred Laliberté (1878-1953), and was unveiled in 1918 at the location of the Hébert farm. The sculpture of Marie Rollet on the monument shows her teaching her three children. Guillaume Couillard (1591-1663) is represented on the back of the monument. He married Marie-Guillemette, Louis' second daughter, in 1621. He is shown with a plow, an implement he introduced to the colony in the spring of 1628.

34. Monument to Monsignor Laval

At the junction of De Buade, Port-Dauphin, and Côte de la Montagne streets, on the slope across the street is the imposing monument dedicated to Monsignor François de Montmorency-Laval, one of the most important religious figures in Québec. Laval was born in 1623 near Chartres, France and studied at the Jesuit Collège de La Flèche in Sarthe. He was consecrated as bishop in 1658, and in 1659 arrived at Québec with the mission of organizing the Catholic church in New France. He founded the Séminaire de Québec in 1663 and the Petit Séminaire in 1668. In 1664 he organized the first parish in the colony, Notre-Dame de Québec, and in 1674 the diocese of Québec. He died in 1708. In 1877 his remains were discovered during construction work in the basement of the cathedral and removed to the crypt in the chapel of the Séminaire de Québec. In 1950 his remains were moved again to a funerary chapel built in the exterior chapel of the Séminaire, and once more in 1993, when the chapel became a part of the Musée du Séminaire, the bishop's remains were moved to the Basilica-Cathedral Notre-Dame de Québec. Monsignor Laval was beatified in 1980 by Pope John Paul II. His statue was unveiled in 1908 to mark the bicentenary of Laval's death. The statue was created by the celebrated sculptor Louis-Philippe Hébert (1850-1917) and the base by Eugène-Étienne Taché (1836-1912). The figure of the woman represents religion, the young boy symbolizes the founding of the Séminaire du Québec, and the Amerindian represents the evangelization and education efforts of the bishop—the angel offers him palm leaves, symbolizing glory.

35. Louis-S. St-Laurent Building

The building behind the statue of Monsignor de Laval is the Louis-S. St-Laurent Building, known as the old Post Office Building (the entrance to the Post Office is at the corner of de la Fort). It was constructed in 1873, then enlarged and embellished between 1913 and 1921. Louis-Stephen St-Laurent (1882-1973) was Canada's Prime Minister from 1948 to 1957.

36. The Legend of the Golden Dog

The modest lintel above the entrance to the Louis-S. St-Laurent Building is carved with the image of a dog gnawing a bone. The lintel was carved in the eighteenth century and it is said to have hung on the Philbert house, which was located on the site of the St-Laurent Building. The lintel is inscribed:

> I am a dog that gnaws his bone,
> I couch and gnaw it all alone—
> A time will come, which is not yet,
> When I'll bite him by whom I'm bit.
> {Trans. from *The Golden Dog*, 1877)

There are numerous interpretations of the legend of the Golden Dog and mysterious inscription. Even now there is no agreement about what the message means. The most common explanation is that the lintel was a tavern sign, probably from France. The message of vengeance appears to be linked to a death at the hands of French Canadian nobleman, François-Xavier Le Gardeur de Repentigny (a military officer) who killed the Frenchman Nicolas Jacquin dit Philibert with a sword because Philibert did not want to have Le Gardeur lodged in his home. The murderer escaped decapitation (by the authorities) by fleeing to New England, and paying 8675 livres and 10 sols to the widow to be pardoned. The simultaneous appearance of the lintel at the time of the killing has provided enough fodder for the legend to flourish, and William Kirby (1817-1906) used it as the title for his novel, *The Golden Dog*, published in 1877.

37. Charles-Baillairgé Stairs

Beside the St-Laurent Building, towards Côte-de-la-Montagne, take the Charles Baillairgé Stairs, built in 1893 to replace an earlier set built in 1841. Turn right on Côte-de-la-Montagne to the Frontenac Stairs.

Tour ends at the foot of the Frontenac Stairs

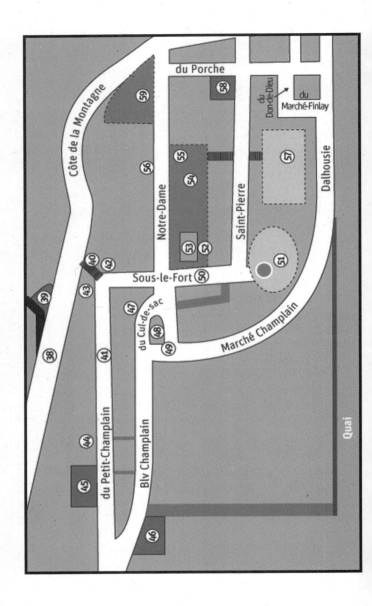

Tour 3

Place Royale and Petit-Champlain Quarter

START: THE FOOT OF THE FRONTENAC STAIRS

38. Prescott Footbridge

You are on Côte-de-la-Montagne, which was laid out in 1623 by Champlain, to connect Upper and Lower Town. It has been called Côte-de-la-Basse-Ville, and then Mountain Hill by the English; its gates were used to control access to Upper Town. The Prescott Gate is at the spot where the pedestrian footbridge connects the Frontenac Stairs with Montmorency Park. Built in 1791 the gate was demolished in 1871 after the English troops left Québec. The gate, according to reports, was built in the medieval style. The Prescott Footbridge was built in 1983.

39. Québec's first cemetery

Go down Côte-de-la-Montagne and across the street just below the ramparts is the location of the first cemetery in the colony—the triangular area marked with a red cross. It was used from the beginning of the colony until 1687 when the Sainte-Anne Cemetery near the Cathédrale Notre-Dame opened. It is said that Champlain's twenty companions who died of scurvy during the winter of 1609 were buried here, along with Marie Rollet (d. 1649), widow of Louis Hébert, the first settler in Québec (#33).

40. Casse-Cou Stairs

Walk down Côte-de-la-Montagne to the Casse-Cou (Break-Neck) Stairs. Before you go down the steps look at the bust of Jean-Paul Lemieux (1904-1990) by Paul Lancz (1998) on your left at the turn. The base displays a painting by Lemieux of the Corpus Christi "procession de la Fête-Dieu" along the Côte-de-la-Montagne. Lemieux was one of Québec's best-known painters; his work often dealt with human solitude in the infinity of nature.

Return to the Casse-Cou Stairs: even though the stairs have existed since 1640, they acquired their name in the nineteenth century, probably because each time they were repaired they became more dangerous. Another version is that it was American visitors to Québec who nicknamed them the Break-Neck Stairs. They have also been called the Basse-Ville (Lower Town) Stairs, the Champlain Stairs, and the Quêteux Stairs. This is the oldest staircase in Québec.

Descend the steps to Basse-Ville (Lower Town). Since the seventeenth century the designations Basse- and Haute-Ville have been used. Basse-Ville was the commercial and industrial sector and Haute-Ville the site of the military fortress, the governor's residence, and the religious communities.

41. Rue du Petit-Champlain

When this street was established in 1685 it was named de Meules (with one "l") after the successor to Intendant (governor) Jean-Talon, Jacques de Meulles de La Source (1650-1703), who was the intendant from 1682 to 1686. It was next called Little Champlain Street, an incorrect translation of Rue du Petit-Champlain which should have been something like "Champlain's Little street". During the nineteenth century it was home to the French and Irish port workers—sailors, stevedores and merchants. It has always been a busy and active street, despite several rock falls (major ones in 1841 and 1889), and even today it is very active. The oldest commercial street in North America, it almost disappeared in 1909 when Prime Minister Wilfrid Laurier's federal government launched a project to build the train station. The station was to be located in the Quartier Petit-Champlain, which would have meant the demolition of the Champlain market and the neighbourhood houses. The market was demolished, but in 1911 the Laurier government fell and the new federal government under Prime Minister Robert Borden abandoned the project. The train station was built near the Louise Basin. Today you can still walk along this historic street and admire the historic houses.

42. La Mailloche Glassworks and Economuseum

On your left at the corner of Petit-Champlain and Sous-le-Fort streets is La Mailloche Glassworks, founded in 1976 by master glass artist Jean Vallières, and located in Old Québec since 1992. This economuseum—store, workshop, and museum—offers visitors a glimpse into the world of glassblowing where you can try out this craft and purchase original works.

Information: 1.866.694.0445

43. Maison Louis-Jolliet

This is the second entrance (the Lower Town one) to the funicular (#6) in the Louis-Jolliet house at 16 Rue du Petit-Champlain. The house was built by Québec's first architect, Claude Baillif (1635-1698), in 1683 for Louis Jolliet, who occupied it until his death in 1700. Jolliet was one of the most important explorers of North America—travelling to the Mississippi with the Jesuit Jacques Marquette (1637-1675) in 1673 in search of a passage to China. Jolliet was one of the first Québécois, born in Québec in 1645, to have left his mark on North America's history. The house was restored in 1946.

Beside the Jolliet House is a small green space with a monument honouring Jolliet, as well as a monument by Lucienne Cornet commemorating the 125th anniversary of the funicular (1879 to 2004).

44. The Cannonball

Continue along Rue du Petit-Champlain, past the charming small shops, and you will come to a cannonball embedded in the wall at number 48, right across from the Cul-de-Sac (Dead End) Stairs. The cannonball is more that 10 centimetres across, painted black, and maintained by the home owners at number 48. There are a number of cannonballs embedded in the walls of Lower and Upper Town, and others are still being found during renovations and repairs. Remember that during the Siege of Québec in 1759, over 40,000 English cannonballs and 10,000 incendiary bombs were fired on Québec (#32).

45. Parc Félix-Leclerc

Walk a bit further along to Félix-Leclerc Park on your right. Félix Leclerc (1914-1988) was one of Québec's most important and much-loved poet-songwriter-singers. He had an international career, especially in France where he made the "La Belle Province" famous. He lived on Île d'Orléans (20 km east of Québec City where Jacques Cartier landed in 1535) for many years, and it inspired many of his songs, including the famous "Tour de l'île". At the end of the park by the cliff is a statue created in 1997 by Hélène Rochette called "Le Souffle de l'île" (Breath of the Island), inspired by the Île d'Orléans. There are often musicians playing in the park; take the time to stop and listen.

The Petit-Champlain Theatre is beside the park. In 1694 when Count Frontenac (#3) wanted to present the play

Tartuffe (1664) by Molière, Québec's bishop, Monsignor de Saint-Vallier, threatened him with excommunication and scuttled the project. Québec experienced the same scandal that had rocked Paris thirty years earlier over the production of this play about false believers. The theatre was renamed the Maison de la Chanson (House of Song), and now presents concerts by francophone artists from around the world.

46. Parc Jean-Paul-Godin, or Parc des Traversiers (Ferryboat Park)

As you walk to the end of Rue du Petit-Champlain you come to the trompe-l'oeil painting, "Petit-Champlain Fresco", of the interior of an early colonial house, which was installed by Murale Création in 2001. Return to Ruelle Magasin-du-Roi or Magasin-du-Roi Lane, which is actually a staircase, and descend to Champlain boulevard and turn left. If you haven't yet eaten and the weather is fine, stop at one of the sunny terrasses. Across from them is the Jean-Paul Godin Park, dedicated to navigation. An enormous anchor and various buoys are on display.

If you want to take the ferry to Lévis on the other side of the river, cross the street to the quays (on Rue des Traversiers). It is an opportunity for an exceptional view of the city. During the winter the trip is unforgettable as the ice breaks across the bow of the ferry. There used to be an ice bridge that crossed the river, but global warming and the rise of water levels ended that. In 1828 a "horse-powered" boat (horses on a treadmill at one end of the boat powered the propeller) built by Charles Poiré transported passengers across the river. Steam-powered boats eventually replaced this unusual conveyance. Today the one kilometre crossing takes 10 minutes on a 700-passenger ferry. Even if you do not make the crossing, be sure to look up from the quay for a superb view of the Château Frontenac. Not to be missed!

Information: 1.877.787.7483

Ferry schedule: Daily, every 20, 30 or 40 minutes (except the first morning crossings, every 20 or 30 minutes) from both Québec and Lévis.

Evenings: Until 2:20 am, every 60 minutes (year-round).

Price: Adults (12 to 64) $2.60, seniors $2.35, children (5 to 11) $1.80, children (under 5) free; plus the cost of vehicle: Car $5.80, Bicycle $2.60.

47. Rue Cul-de-Sac

Make your way to the corner of Marché-Champlain and Cul-de-Sac. This protected cove, which is now solid land, was the site of the first naval dockyards—the tides actually rose to Rue St-Pierre and into the cove.

48. Maison Chevalier (Chesnay and Frérot Houses)

At the corner of Marché-Champlain and Cul-de-Sac streets is the Chevalier House, really three houses: the first at the corner of Cul-de-Sac and Notre-Dame is the Chesnay House, originally built by Bertrand Chesnay de Garenne in the seventeenth century and entirely rebuilt in 1959. Chesnay also constructed the oldest of the three houses, the one in the centre, named after its second owner, Thomas Frérot.

The third house, the actual Chevalier House, was built by Baptiste Chevalier in 1752, and rebuilt in 1762 after a major fire. The imposing construction is typical of New France's urban architecture. The house, sometimes called the Hôtel Chevalier, was the London Coffee House Inn for more than a century. It was frequented by sailors and butchers. It is interesting to note that the entrance is actually located at the rear of the original building and this was restored in 1959. The lower windows of the original façade were used to move merchandise in directly from the quays that were right beside the houses. The interior of the Chevalier House is now furnished with artifacts from the Musée de la Civilization's collection. (The Musée owns the buildings.)

Guided tours: Approx. 30 minutes. Information available at the Centre d'interprétation Place Royale (#56)

Information: 418.646.3167

Hours: June 24 to September 4: daily 9:30 am to 5:00 pm. May 5 to June 23, September 5 to October 15, and December 13 to January 1: Tuesday to Sunday 10:00 am to 5:00 pm. Other times of year: Saturday and Sunday 10:00 am to 5:00 pm outside these periods

Fee: Free

49. Patrimoine Vivant Atelier

Through the burgundy-coloured door to the left of the entrance to the Chevalier House are the building's vaults. Québec artisans in this living heritage workshop sell works that are produced using traditional methods including candles, knits, and lace. The artisans are friendly and offer unique creations.

Hours: Open during the summer Friday, Saturday, and Sunday 10:30 am to 4:30 pm

Fee: Free

50. Rue Sous-le-Fort

Take Rue Notre-Dame to Rue Sous-le-Fort (Below the Fort) which leads to the funicular. Notre-Dame and Sous-le-Fort are the oldest "official" streets in the city. The 1640 *Plan de Québec* by surveyor Jean Bourdon (1601-1688) shows these two "streets"—they were paths, really—and several other unnamed paths. Sous-le-Fort was originally called des Roches, but was renamed because it is located directly below Fort Saint-Louis, 60 metres above.

51. Batterie royale (Royal Battery)

Turn right and go down Rue Sous-le-Fort a short way to

Passage de la batterie. This section of the battlements is a reconstruction.

Go back along Sous-le-Fort to the end of the street, almost facing Rue St-Pierre, to the Batterie royale, which was part of Québec's defence system during the Siege of Québec in 1759. In 1691 Frontenac had Claude Baillif (1635-1698) and Jean-Baptiste-Louis Franquelin (1651-1712) build this earthen rampart for the battery of cannons to be used against the English (#32). The spot was called Pointe-aux-Roches (Rocky Point) and in 1763 it became a landing stage—the river was much higher then. During the nineteenth century the Batterie royale disappeared. The site was restored to the 1691 plans in 1977. There are ten cannons, replicas of French cannons, donated by Raymond Barre, prime minister of France in the 1970s. The coat of arms, located above the entrance to the Battery, is also a reproduction. The original was taken to England where it stayed for decades, finally being returned to Québec's Hôtel-de-ville (city hall) in the 1960s.

52. Rue des Pains-Bénits

Return along Rue Sous-le-Fort to the tiny Rue des Pains-Bénits (street of Blessed Breads). Its name arises from the traditional blessing of bread after the Siege of Paris in 464, during which Geneviève, a young woman (who was to become a saint and the object of a devotional cult) procured grain for the starving citizens. Sainte Geneviève is called upon for protection from famine, and at the Notre-Dame-des-Victoires Church her day, January 3rd, is celebrated by a blessing of the breads.

53. Notre-Dame-des-Victoires Church

Take Rue des Pains-Bénits to Notre-Dame-des-Victoires Church (Our Lady of the Victories) on Place Royale. This attractive little church was built in 1688 by Claude Baillif

(1635-1698) on the foundations of Samuel de Champlain's first residence (#5), which had been constructed in 1608, the first European building in Québec. In the basement of the church you can still see one of the trading post's original walls and a turret. Excavations were recently undertaken, and the paving stones in front of the church—which were reconstructed in 1990—give a feel of the original site. This church, dedicated to the Infant Jesus, is an auxiliary to the Notre-Dame de Québec Cathedral-Basilica which was built under Monsignor Laval (#34). In 1690 the church became Notre-Dame-de-la-Victoire when the governor of New France, Frontenac (#3), defeated the troops of British Admiral William Phips' fleet who had landed at Beauport across from Québec. In 1711 the church was renamed Notre-Dame-*des-Victoires* to include the commemoration of the sinking of Admiral Sir Hovenden Walker's British fleet during a storm, as he was about to attack the city. The two frescos, on either side of the statue of Notre-Dame-des-Victoires on the high altar in the church, are by Jean-Marie Tardivel and depict scenes of these victories. In 1723 the church was enlarged, adding the Sainte-Geneviève Chapel, but in 1759 the church was destroyed during the Siege of Québec. It was rebuilt between 1763 and 1766 by Jean Baillairgé (1726-1805); the interior decoration was completed between 1854 and 1857 and is attributed to Raphael Giroux. In 1929 the building was declared an historic site by the Québec government.

If you go into the church do not miss the votive offering hanging from the vault of the nave. Nicknamed "Friendly Martha", it is a model of the *Brézé*, the ship that carried the Marquis de Tracy and the Carignan-Salières regiment to Québec in 1665. The marquis offered the model to the church in thanksgiving to God for their safe and healthy arrival. The model was lost for more than two centuries, but was rediscovered and hung in the nave in 1995. The church also contains paintings which were removed from several churches in Paris during the French Revolution, which Abbé Philippe Desjardins acquired. They were brought to Québec between 1817 and 1821.

On Sundays during the summer there is a sung mass from 10:30 am to noon, and guided visits are also available. Information: 418.692.1650

54. Place Royale

Place Royale is considered to be the cradle of French civilization in America, but long before the arrival of Europeans the site was occupied by Amerindians who fished and traded there. In 1608 Samuel de Champlain built the l'Abitation, the Habitation, three living quarters protected by a palisade. By 1680 the area now known as the Petit-Champlain quarter was filled with successful businesses that flourished until 1759. Place Royale quickly became Place-du-Marché, and Québec became the main port of entry between Europe and New France. After the takeover of Québec by British troops in 1759, Place Royale was completely destroyed, then later rebuilt. The Place was an important commercial hub; for more than 50 years Québec was Britain's largest port in North America. During the second half of the nineteenth century Québec's commercial importance shrank and even though Place Royale held on to some economic power, by the 1950s the quarter had declined enormously. It regained its original name in 1957, and since 1970 a restoration and business plan has turned Place-Royale into the jewel it is today.

Worth noting: there are 27 hidden vaulted cellars under Place Royale that are among the oldest in Québec. The majority were built during the eighteenth century for protection during fires and bombardments, to prevent theft, and to provide food storage. You can visit the cellars from the Place-Royale Interpretation Centre where you can get a feel for daily life during the eighteenth century. There are also vaulted cellars at the Maison Chevalier, the Musée de la civilization (#69), and the Musée du Jade near the statue of Louis XIV.

55. Statue of Louis XIV

This statue in the centre of Place-Royale is a copy of a marble statue at Versailles, carved by Antoine Coysevox (1640-1720), and a gift of French cabinet minister Maurice Bokanowski in 1928. It has had a complicated history: there had been a statue of Louis XIV in the Place in 1686, but it was soon removed following a request from the merchants. At the beginning of the twentieth century a fountain was installed, but in 1931 the new statue was erected. Once again, it was removed, in part because taxi drivers had a difficult time negotiating the Place—cars were allowed on the Place until quite recently. Regardless, the statue was re-installed in 1948.

56. Centre d'interprétation de Place-Royale (Place-Royale Interpretation Centre)

The Interpretation Centre was built on the site of the Hazeur and Smith houses (1637), and opened in 1999. There are exhibits, guided visits, and a multimedia presentation to introduce the history of the Place with dynamic activities for children including disguises, mysteries, and a range of other possibilities. Even more intriguing are the workshops, which sometimes occur outside the Centre where visitors and passersby are invited by the costumed guide to learn about some facet of life in an earlier time including naval life, knowledge about medicinal plants or knots, tobacco consumption, the life of the *coureurs des bois* (unlicensed fur traders), and so on. The Centre also organizes events in the Place: the traditional musicians who play during the summer, the autumn market, and a presentation about Christmas in earlier times.

Information: 418.646.3167, 1.866.710.8031

Hours: June 24 to September 2: daily 9:30 am to 5:00 pm.
Sept. 5 to June 23: Tuesday to Sunday 10:00 am to 5:00 pm

Multimedia Presentation: Daily, on the half-hour from 10:30 am to 4:30 pm

Guided Visits: During the summer at 11:15 am, 1:30 pm and 4:00 pm

Fee: Adults $5.00, seniors $4.50, students $3.50, children Free

Free admission: On Tuesdays from November 1 to May 31, also from 10:00 am to 12 noon every Saturday in January and February

57. Place de Paris

Take the stairway in front of the statue of Louis XIV down towards the river, past Rue St-Pierre, and continue straight along to the small park, the Place de Paris (formerly the Finlay Market). The Place was inaugurated in 1988 and named for the large white marble statue of Paris created by French sculptor Jean-Pierre Raynauld (b. 1939). Called "Dialogue with History", it was a gift of the city of Paris to the city of Québec. One of the possible interpretations is that the piece represents our vast landscape and time—a dialogue between the past, the present, and the future; an eternal link between France and Québec. This modern work has been somewhat controversial among residents of Quebec City.

58. Parc de l'UNESCO

Go back up the de la Place lane and turn right on Rue St-Pierre, which was the financial quarter of Québec that until 1850 rivaled Montréal as the economic capital of the colony. The city then suffered a serious decline—its importance as a port and its prosperity diminished.

A bit further along St-Pierre is UNESCO Park, a dream-come-true for kids—filled with wooden games and toys. This is a required stop for children. Around 1651 this was the location of the first general store operated by the Mathurin Gagnon and his brothers Jean and Pierre from Tourouvre, France. There is a painting of the store on the wall to your left. The Association internationale des études québécoises (International Association of Québec Studies) is further along in the park on the left.

59. Parc de la Cetière

Follow Rue du Porche, keeping to your left until Notre-Dame. You are now at the Parc de la Cetière. It is named after the colonist Florent de la Cetière, who lived right beside this spot. The wall of the house to your left sports the "Fresco of Québec," created by a group of artists from Québec and Lyon known collectively as Cité de la Creation in 1999. This trompe d'oeil painting is 420 square metres (4,520 sq. ft.). Many historical and contemporary figures are part of the depiction of the four seasons. Look for Jacques Cartier, Samuel de Champlain, Marie de l'Incarnation, Count Frontenac, Louis Jolliet, and Félix Leclerc.

On the right are the ruins of old houses. Read the information panels to find out about the houses and the many people who occupied them over the centuries. There are often musical concerts in the park; information is available at the Centre d'interprétation Place-Royale (#56).

End of tour at Parc de la Cetière.

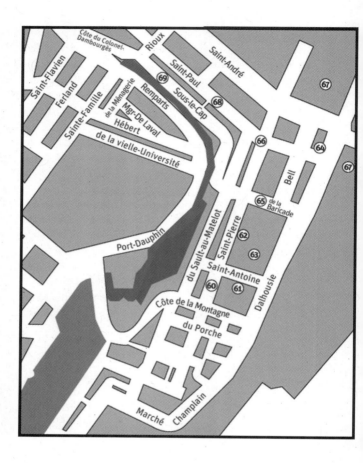

Tour 4

Rue St-Paul and Museum of Civilization

START: PARC DE LA CETIÈRE

60. Rue St-Pierre

Walk down Côte de la Montagne and turn left onto Rue St-Pierre. In earlier times St-Pierre was the border between dry land and the river, but merchants gradually created new land with infill and constructed their homes there. At the end of the seventeenth and beginning of the eighteenth centuries, Charles Aubert de la Chesnaye and Philippe Gauthier de Comporté, two wealthy merchants in furs, oils, and dried fish, built their wharf at this spot. At the beginning of the nineteenth century, the merchants, fearing cholera epidemics, moved to Upper Town along the Grande Allée (#111), among other locations. Banks and insurance companies moved in along St-Pierre, making it Québec City's equivalent to Wall Street. During the 1960s the banks left and restoration work began, returning the street to its earlier luster.

61. Auberge Saint-Antoine

At 58 Rue St-Pierre look up at the *mascarons*—carved grotesque faces or masks, vestiges of an earlier, wealthier time. Check out the Auberge St-Antoine at 10 St-Antoine on Îlot Hunt. Îlot Hunt was the location of wharfs and then cannon batteries before Jean Maillou built his house there in 1725.

The house was partially destroyed in the war of 1759, but the walls were saved. In 1822 John Chillas, a master cooper, bought the site and built a warehouse—today the restaurant *Le Panache*. The site was abandoned for many years until the Price family (#75) purchased it and opened the restaurant in 1992. The uniqueness of the inn is that the ruins and artifacts found during archeological digs have been integrated into the modern décor. Take a look in the inn's bar.

62. Maison Estèbe

Number 92 Rue St-Pierre is the Estèbe House, which, like the Chevalier House (# 48), is among the treasures belonging to the Musée de la civilisation (Museum of Civilization). It was built in 1751 for Guillaume Estèbe and his wife Élisabeth-Marie Thivierge—and their 14 future children. The house is an enormous classical French-style building with 21 rooms and eight fireplaces that somehow survived the war of 1759. After the Conquest the Estèbe family abandoned the house and returned to France. The house remained a private residence until the nineteenth century when various businesses took it over. In 1959 it was classified as an historical monument, and in 1984 the museum acquired it. The house adjoins the museum, and the museum boutique is located in its vaults. You can also see the ancient well.

63. Musée de la civilisation

Beside the Estèbe House, at 80 Rue St-Pierre, is the entrance to the Museum of Civilization, which opened in 1988. Across the street from the Museum entrance is the Auberge Saint-Pierre. You can see the name "Québec Assurance Building" inscribed in stone on the façade,—a reminder of an earlier time and a different neighbourhood. The museum houses two permanent exhibits, *Le temps des Québécois* (The People of Québec: Then and Now) and *Nous, les premières nations*

(Encounter with the First Nations). There are also numerous temporary exhibits, always interesting and often surprising, as much for their subject matter as for their presentation. The museum is very dynamic and there are many activities; among them are creative workshops for children. Visit the vaulted cellars of the Pagé-Quercy House, all that remains of the house built by Guillaume Pagé dit Quercy, between 1695 and 1713.

Even if you do not visit the museum walk around the foyer (and take the opportunity to use the washrooms). The architecture—it was designed by Moshe Safdie—melds the traditional and the modern very successfully. The installation *La débâcle* of bleached concrete paving stones in a cantilevered pattern that forms the base of a pool was created by Montreal artist Astri Reusch. It symbolizes the spring breakup of the river ice which used to cover this spot.

Information: 418.643.2158, 1.866.710.8031

Hours: June 24 to September 4: daily 9:30 am to 6:30 pm. September 5 to June 23: Tues. to Sunday 10:00 am to 5:00 pm

Guided visits: Check at the information desk

Fees: Adults $10.00, seniors $9.00, students $7.00, children free

64. *Ex Machina*

Walk across the lobby of the museum and leave through the Rue Dalhousie exit. Turn left on Dalhousie towards Rue de la Barricade. *Ex Machina* (109 Dalhousie), situated in what was once Firehouse No. 5, is an artistic production centre that was founded in 1993 by Robert Lepage, the internationally known theatre director. It is a multidisciplinary company that includes actors, producers, directors, designers, musicians, computer graphic designers, video artists, and acrobats. The firehouse was built on the ruins of Québec City's first stock exchange which was established in 1828.

65. Rue de la Barricade

Turn left on Rue de la Barricade. Between St-Pierre and Du Sault-au-Matelot streets there is a plaque commemorating the failed attacks on Québec by troops from the Thirteen Colonies in December 1775. At that time the people of the Thirteen Colonies were extremely frustrated by the taxes imposed on them by the British government and their campaign for military control included an invasion of Québec, which had come under British control after the Conquest of 1759. The American invaders under Generals Richard Montgomery (1736-1775) and Benedict Arnold (1741-1801) launched the attack on the British troops of Governor Guy Carleton (Lord Dorchester, 1724-1808) during the night on December 31. The first barricade, at the corner of Côte de la Canoterie and Côte du Colonel-Damourgès, was breeched, but the second at Sault-au-Matelot and de la Barricade streets held. The attacking militia troops were exhausted—Arnold's troops had marched from New England, and Montgomery's troops had fought in the Montréal area before arriving at Québec. The invaders assumed that the French Canadian militia, which had battled the British fifteen years before, would support them, but instead they fought with the British to defend their homeland against another invasion.

66. Place de la F.A.O. (F.A.O. Plaza)

Continue to Rue du Sault-au-Matelot and turn right. According to legend the street got its name when a sailor fell from the cliff at this spot, but the street has had its name since the early days of the colony when the word "sault" was used rather that "chute" for "waterfall"—there was a waterfall here during the seventeenth century.

The F.A.O. (Food and Agriculture Organization of the United Nations) Square is at the junction of St-Paul, St-Pierre, and Du Sault-au-Matelot streets. The sculpture *La Vivrière* (literally, the food producer) by Richard Purdy in the centre of the plaza commemorates the 50th anniversary of the founding of the United Nations in 1945. It represents the perpetual cycle of life and human survival in the form of a produce-laden ship under sail. The surrounding paving stones recall the water and waves that once reached this point.

If you want to go to the Vieux-Port (Old Port), turn right onto Rue St-Paul.

67. Le Vieux-Port (The Old Port)

This walk is optional—it extends the tour quite a bit, but it is worth it, especially if you are interested in navigation and things nautical. Since the beginning of the colony the port has played a crucial role in the development of the city, and it prospered well into the nineteenth century. First there was the fur trade, then lumber, grain, and other raw materials. By the end of the nineteenth century, the port was in slow decline because of changes in the transportation system—steam boats, railways, and the development of canals along the St. Lawrence River made Montréal the commercial hub of the province. Since the early 1970s the Vieux-Port has experienced major renovations—pleasure craft now dock here, and cruise ships visit at Pointe-à-Carcy. This is a good spot to embark on a tour by water to see Québec from another vantage point. There are many tours available lasting from one and a half to seven hours, with or without a meal, day or evening, for prices between $27.00 and $65.00 per adult. The regular season is from May to October.

Croisières AML
Information: 1.800.563.4643

Croisière Le Coudrier
Information: 1.800.600.5554

Croisières Groupe Dufour
Information: 1.800.436.5250

If you want to visit the Vieux-Port, walk along Rue St-Paul and cross Dalhousie to the pedestrian walkway between the two buildings near the ferry terminal. L'Agora, an entertainment venue, is in the Vieux-Port along with the Pointe-à-Carcy, a green space with an unimpeded view of the river. Walk by the Customs Building (built in 1856) and the Naval Museum of Québec, where the main events and conflicts of Québec's past are the context for its maritime history, from colonial times to the present.
Information: 418.694.5387

Walk towards the Louise Basin, past the many pleasure boats. During the 1880s a wharf was built in the St. Charles River estuary which connected with the Vieux-Port. The Louise Basin was named in honour of Princess Louise, one of Queen Victoria's daughters. The Centre d'interprétation du Vieux-Port de Québec is, unfortunately, closed until 2009 to make room for Québec's 400th anniversary celebrations. Further along take a look at the locally grown produce in the Marché du Vieux-Port—you can also rent a bicycle here.
Cyclo Services
Information: 418.692.4052, 1.877.692.4050
Hours: Daily from May 1 to October 31
Fee: $12.00 per person, per bike

68. Rue St-Paul

At the Place F.A.O. (#66) turn right on St-Paul towards the Côte du Colonel-Dambourgès (Dambourgès was a member of the Legislative Assembly of Lower Canada). On St-Paul there are a number of enticing shops and terraces to stop in for a coffee, as well as antiques dealers, art galleries, and boutiques. The street is lined with trees and makes for an agreeable stroll.

69. Rue Sous-le-Cap

If you take the Passage de la Demi-Lune to your left, you come out on Sous-le-Cap (Under the Cape), an unusual little street that is more like a lane. It was known as Ruelle des Chiens (Dog Alley) and appeared as such on an early eighteenth century map. For a long time it was considered unsavory—sailors' women and prostitutes lived there.

Turn right on the street and look at the back yards on your right and on your left the sheds which are attached to buildings by walkways. This maze of walkways, stairs, balconies, clotheslines, and flowerboxes is quite unique. Perched on the towering rock, the ramparts rise high over the "Cap". It is easy to appreciate the terms "Upper" and "Lower" Town.

Continue to the end of Sous-le-Cap to the Côte du Colonel-Dambourgès, then turn left and climb the hill. At Côte de la Canoterie (named because the Jesuits used to tie their canoes just below, close to the St. Charles River) cross the street and climb the wooden staircase to Rue des Remparts.

End: Des Remparts and St-Flavien streets

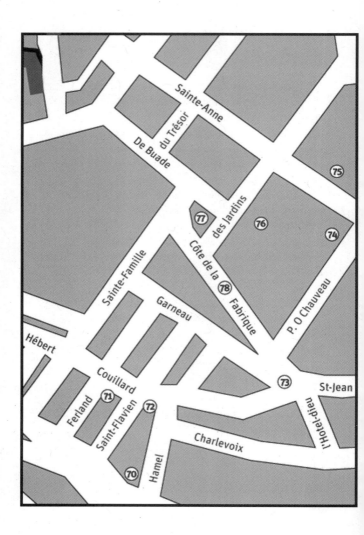

74. Place des Frères éducateurs
(Monument to the Teaching Brothers)

Walk along Rue de la Côte de la Fabrique and turn right onto Rue Pierre-Olivier-Chaveau. Chauveau (1820-1890) was the premier of Québec from 1867 to 1873 in the first post-Confederation government. At the corner of Pierre-Olivier-Chauveau and Ste-Anne streets there is a monument to all of the Brothers who devoted their lives to teaching. The sculpture, "Envol" (Taking Flight), was created by Jules Lasalle in 1999. There is a short text by him engraved on the base of the statue which explains the symbolism of the piece.

75. Price Building

Take Rue Ste-Anne to your left. Across the street the office tower is the Price Building, built in 1929. It was the first tall building in Québec and the only one in Old Québec. It was built by the Price Brothers paper company as their head office. William Price arrived in Québec in 1810 and quickly became prominent in the newly-important forestry industry, thanks to the continental blockade imposed by Napoleon on the export of Baltic timber to England. The company concentrated on sawmills and pulp and paper production, and, after a series of amalgamations, became Abitibi Consolidated, one of the largest newsprint producers in the world. Price House accommodates the official residence of the Premier of Québec, as well as the offices of the Caisse de dépot et placement du Québec, the huge manager of public pension plans in Québec. Just beside the building is the Clarendon Hotel, built on the site of the old Hay Market.

76. Hôtel de ville (City Hall)

The building you have just walked around is Québec's city hall and its park. Go to the main entrance on Rue des Jardins. The city hall is on the site of the former Jesuit College which was built in 1635. The College burned down in 1640 and was rebuilt between 1647 and 1650. In 1725 the College was expanded, but after the Conquest in 1759 the English took possession of the buildings and by 1765 they had converted it into a barracks. Slightly damaged from the bombardment during the Siege of Québec in 1759, it was in reasonable condition. When the English troops left, it had suffered from hard use. The building was partially demolished in 1807, and then entirely in 1878. Near the entrance to the Hôtel de ville, you can see the remains of the original building—three of the building stones from the entrance pediment bearing the letters IHS, sometimes translated as Iesus hominum salvator (Jesus, saviour of humanity) or as an abbreviation of Jesus' name. The Hôtel de ville was built in 1895-1896 according to the plans of architect Georges-Emile Tanguay (1858-1923). From the triangular pediment of the Hôtel de ville flies Québec City's flag: the *Don-de-Dieu* was Champlain's ship, and the crenelated border symbolizes the fortifications. The motto of the city is "Don de Dieu feray valoir" ("Gift of God I will make thee worthy").

77. Place de l'Hôtel de ville (City Hall Square)

In front of the Hôtel de ville there is a small square, formerly the Notre-Dame Market Square, with a statue of Cardinal Elzéar-Alexandre Taschereau (1820-1898) created by the French sculptor Vermare and cast in bronze in Paris, then installed in Québec in 1923. Cardinal Taschereau was the first Canadian cardinal (1886); he was the Superior of the Séminaire du Québec, rector of Laval University, and in 1847, provided aid to the Irish typhoid victims at the Grosse-Île quarantine site downstream from Île d'Orléans.

78. Côte de la Fabrique

Walk down the de la Fabrique hill back to Livernois Square

at the junction of St-Jean, de la Fabrique, and Couillard streets. Since the beginning of the colony Côte de la Fabrique has been a path along a riverbed leading to the St. Charles River. It appears on a maps dating from 1660, and is so named because it traverses the "factory fief" of the city. The Librairie générale française bookshop, at 10 Côte de la Fabrique close to Ste-Famille, was founded in 1971. It has a large selection of books on the region of Québec (along with Librairie Pantoute at 1100 St-Jean). Another bookstore, Librairie Crémazie, which was run by the celebrated Québec poet Octave Crémazie (1827-1879), was once located at 32 de la Côte. Still on Côte de la Fabrique is Simons department store (#104), formerly the Empire Cinema, and later Madame Belley's Museum. Madame Belley was an eccentric, well known during the 1960s.

End of tour: St-Jean and Hôtel-Dieu streets (Place du Livernois)

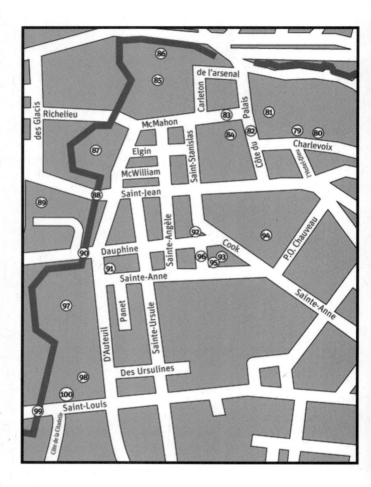

Tour 6

Hôtel-Dieu and the St-Jean, Kent and St-Louis Gates

START: CORNER OF ST-JEAN AND HÔTEL-DIEU (PLACE DU LIVERNOIS)

79. Marie-Catherine de St-Augustin Monument

Take Rue Hôtel-Dieu along to Charlevois to the statue honouring Marie-Catherine de St-Augustin (1632-1668), born Catherine de Longpré de Saint-Sauveur-le-Vicomte in Normandy. The statue shows her leaning against a pillar representing the monastery of Bayeux which she entered in 1644 and left in 1648 for New France. She was the co-founder of the Catholic Church in Canada, embracing Augustinian goals. She devoted her life to the poor and sick, and was beatified in 1989 by John Paul II.

80. Monastère des Augustines de l'Hôtel-Dieu and the Musée des Augustines
(Monastery of Hôtel-Dieu of Québec and the Augustinian Museum)

The Augustinian Monastery of Hôtel-Dieu of Québec is just in front of you. In 1637 Marie-Madeleine de Vienerot, duchess of Aiguillon (1604-1675), a niece of Cardinal Richelieu, signed a contract with the Augustinian Hospitalières du monastère de Dieppe (Normandy) to found a hospital in New

France. Construction work began in 1637 and continued until 1646. In 1639 three nuns arrived in Québec and opened the first hospital in North America. They went on to found eleven other hospitals, but the Hôtel-Dieu of Québec remains the most important, as well as being one of the oldest monasteries of Québec. Starting in 1695 the hospital was enlarged using the plans of François de la Joue (c1656-1719). A fire destroyed the addition in 1755, but it was rebuilt on the foundations. The monastery adjoining the hospital is located in the oldest part of the hospital buildings. The cloister was built in 1757 and was used by the English as a barracks and hospital for their soldiers after the Conquest. The Augustinians regained possession of their building in 1784, and the church was constructed between 1800 and 1803. In 1825 the first hospital not attached to the monastery was built. You cannot see these old buildings from the street, but you can see the Chapel which was constructed in 1931. The museum at 32 Rue Charlevois is administered by the Augustinian sisters, and is located in the newest part of the complex. It was opened in 1958 and its exhibits include many articles evocative of the Augustinian mission, life in Québec since the seventeenth century, and the evolution of medicine in Québec. Today the hospital belongs to the state, but the Augustinians remain the owners of the monastery.

Information: 418.692.2492

Guided tours: Available in English and French

Hours: Monday: closed. Tuesday to Saturday: 9:30 am to noon; 1:30 pm to 5:00 pm. Sunday: 1:30 pm to 5:00 pm

Fee: Free

81. Hôtel-Dieu

Continue along Rue Charlevois and on your left towards Côte du Palais is the Fresque de l'Hôtel-Dieu de Québec. This large trompe-d'oeil fresco was created by Murale Création in 2003, and depicts the development and mission of this hospital, built in 1644 on this site, and which has always provided health care that has evolved with the times. The most recent addition is a fifteen-storey building constructed in 1954. Still today, the Hôtel-Dieu is a hospital affiliated with the Université Laval's medical school and is engaged in medical research. As a bizarre side-note, between 1800 and 1845, the hospital received a total of 1375 children who were homeless or who had been born out of wedlock. They were housed in a tower—more like a circular closet—at the Hôtel-Dieu. The children's tower no longer exists, but in 1866 a memorial to the children was placed in front of the door to the Augustinian Monastery near the gate. Turn right on Côte du Palais to the main entrance to the hospital.

82. Côte du Palais

The hillside that is the Côte du Palais, named in the nineteenth century, refers back to the Intendant's Palace (where the road led) of the French Regime. In 1663 Louis XIV instituted the position of Intendant to manage the problems of the colony (mostly underpopulation and under-funding). Jean Talon (1625-1694) was the second Intendant of New France, but the first to actually come to Québec. He instituted a policy to promote population growth, in part with "Les filles du Roy", young, single women who were sent to the colony with a dowry from the king to marry single colonists, the vast majority of whom were men. Between 1663 and 1673, 770 young women arrived, and within a few years the colony's population had tripled.

83. Rue McMahon

From Côte du Palais turn left onto Rue McMahon (the Salvation Army is on the corner), named for the second Anglophone Catholic priest of Québec. This is the beginning of the Irish neighbourhood, and many of the buildings are a testament to their historical presence. In 1861 Québec had 60,000 residents; 35,200 were Francophones, 24,800 were Anglophones of which 16,800 were Irish, 28 per cent of the population.

84. Old St. Patrick's Church and Saint Patrick's School (in the Irish Quarter)

To your left on Rue McMahon is the façade of the old St. Patrick's Church—the Irish community's oldest Catholic church—built in 1832 under the direction of Thomas Baillairgé (1791-1859). Before it was built, the Irish Catholics were allowed to use the French Catholic churches, the Basilica and the Notre-Dame-des-Victoires Church in Place Royale. St. Patrick's Church was used until 1959, and has been classed as an historic monument. In 1970 a fire destroyed all but three walls which are now part of the new annex to Hôtel-Dieu, housing the hospital's cutting-edge medical research centre. At 6 Rue St-Stanislas you can see the presbytery and Father McMahon's manse, as well as the former Saint Brigid's Home (a senior's residence and orphanage), just beside the old St. Patrick's Church site. The church is now located outside the walls of Old Québec. Across the street at 10 St-Stanislas is the second St. Patrick's School—the first was on Rue des Glacis—built in 1883 and used until 1919.

The monument at the corner of St-Stanislas and McMahon was a gift from Ireland to the city of Québec to commemorate the help offered by Québecers to Irish immigrants who arrived in the mid-nineteenth century at the time of Ireland's Great Famine. Thousands of Irish came to Québec, often under horrible circumstances and in dire straits. Many died during the crossing, and more succumbed while quarantined at Grosse-Île, 46 km (26 miles) downstream from Québec.

85. Parc-de-l'Artillerie (Artillery Park)

The park just behind the Irish monument is Artillery Park (2 Rue d'Auteuil), so named for the presence during the nineteenth century of the Royal Regiment of Artillery. It is a strategic defensive location, providing protection against any possible attack from the St. Charles River which encircles this part of the city. There are many buildings in the park which you can visit: the Redoute Dauphine (1712), the large white building positioned at the bottom of the slope; the Officers' Quarters (1818), which is the charming small house facing Rue McMahon across from the Redoute Dauphine; the Arsenal Foundry (1903) is a bit further along. Start your visit at the Foundry. At McMahon and d'Auteuil streets there is an information plaque; walk between the buildings—the entrance is to your right at the end. The entrance fee includes a visit to the three buildings where costumed guides to welcome you and answer your questions.

Information: 418.648.4205 / Toll free: 1.888.773.8888

Hours: Summer months only: April to mid-October

Tours last 60 minutes

Fees: Adults $4.00, seniors $3.50, youth $2.00, family $10.00

La Fonderie (The Foundry)

The Foundry was built on the site of an earlier powder magazine. The famous scale model of Québec was constructed in 1808 by Jean-Baptiste Duberger (1767-1821), surveyor, and John By (1779-1836), engineer. (Many affirm that it was Duberger alone who built it.) The model was a personal project by the two men, but it was used to plan new installations to improve the existing fortifications. It was built on a scale of 1:300, and was 10 metres (33 feet) long, but was reduced by almost half after it was taken to England in 1810. It was returned to Québec in 1908 and has been on display since 1979.

Dauphine Redoubt

After you have visited the Foundry return to Rue McMahon and to the Dauphine Redoubt, which was built between 1712 and 1749 by Gaspard-Joseph Chaussegros de Léry, the chief engineer of the colony. It is the second oldest military construction in the city and was used until 1871. The four storey building has vaults, a blockhouse, a typical early nineteenth century kitchen, a luxurious English officers' mess, and the Superintendent of the Arsenal's parlor. There are massive buttresses and vaults. You can get a good idea of what military life was like during this period—everything is arranged to create the impression that the soldiers are still present.

Le logis des officiers (The Officers' Quarters)

The Officers' Quarters' and garden are located beside the Redoubt in a former bakery which was converted for the British officers. Its furnishings are in the style of the 1830s, and it is again possible to get a taste of the lifestyle of the officers and their families.
Open in July and August

86. Ancienne caserne de soldats (The Barracks)

The earliest barracks in Québec were built at the bottom of the hill during the eighteenth century during the French Regime, under the direction of Chaussegros de Léry. Before that time the soldiers were billetted with the townspeople, but the population was unhappy with the situation and the authorities decided to build barracks. They were 160 metres (525 feet) long and two storeys high, and could house 200 to 400 soldiers, in dirty and over-crowded conditions. It is not possible to visit, but you can walk around to the back of the buildings and read the information panels for further information. French troops and then British troops were

Séminair de Québec (#28)

billetted there until 1871 when the buildings were converted into workshops and foundries where shells and cartridges were manufactured until 1964.

The parade ground in front of the barracks was used for military exercises, and today during the months of July and August there is a free demonstration of musket drills at 1:15 and 3:15 pm.

In Artillery Park, go to the corner of the fortifications at the back of the park to the pentagon-shaped Palais Redoubt of earlier times. The Redoubt was the quarters of the hangman—somewhat removed from the city and her citizens. There are information plaques throughout the park with as much information as you might wish for—and there are many cannons (#32).

87. *Les Dames de Soie*, Économusée de la poupée (Doll Economuseum)

Return towards the Foundry, and right by the entrance is Les Dames de Soie (the Silk Ladies) in the south wing of the gun carriage warehouse (the carriages were intricate wooden structures designed to support the cannons). The warehouse construction started in 1815 to protect the gun carriages from humidity and bad weather before they were deployed. Today the Doll Ecomuseum, part store, part museum, and part factory, offers an original boutique where you can buy porcelain dolls that were created on the premises and elsewhere. You can order the doll of your dreams. There is an interpretation centre with a history of dolls through the ages and of Les Dames de Soie. You can watch the artisans constructing dolls, and make your own doll too. It's an interesting concept that ties shopping and learning together.
Information: 418.692.1516 / Toll free: 1.877.692.1516
Hours: Monday to Saturday 11:00 am to 5:00 pm
Fee: Free ($4.00 for a guided tour)

88. Porte Saint-Jean (Saint-Jean Gate)

When you leave the store you can climb the stairs that pass under the St-Jean Gate to get a good view of the neighbourhood. Then go down Rue St-Jean, named for Jean Bourdon (1601-1668), surveyor for King Louis XIV, who devised the Plan de Québec in 1640, and lived on the street. It has remained a commercial location for many years, and you can shop both inside and outside the walls.

Go through the St-Jean Gate. The first gate was built in 1693 by Boisberthelot de Beaucours (c1662-1750), but it was a part of an inner wall of the main wall (next to Rue Ste-Ursule). It was demolished in 1720, and rebuilt in 1757 on the ramparts by Gaspard-Joseph Chaussegros de Léry (1721-1797), and once again demolished in 1898. The gate was rebuilt in 1939.

The gate commemorates the fact that Jean-Eustache Lanoullier de Boisclerc, New France's chief road commissioner, left Québec on August 5, 1734 for Montreal and inaugurated the Chemin du Roy, the first carriage-passable road between Montreal and Québec. (Today it is Route 138). It was 280 km (174 miles) long and 7.4 metres (24 feet) wide—an impressive accomplishment for the time. Until the King's Road was constructed, the river was the only link between the two cities.

89. Place d'Youville

Just outside the Saint-Jean Gate is Place d'Youville—during the summer a site for many activities, and in the winter, a skating rink. The sculpture by Alfred Laliberté (1878-1953) is called *Les Muses*; it was a gift from the government of Québec to the city of Québec on the occasion of the 375th anniversary of the city's founding.

On your right at the edge of the square is the Cabaret du Capitole, an important concert venue built in 1903, and to your left is the Palais Montcalm, another concert hall built in 1932. Return to the Old Town through the Saint-Jean Gate and turn right on Rue d'Auteuil.

At the corner of Saint-Jean and d'Auteuil is the famous restaurant Chantauteuil, a favorite gathering place for the artistic community of Québec city since the 1970s.

90. Porte Kent (Kent Gate)

Walk along Rue d'Auteuil to Dauphine to the Kent Gate on your right. The gate was built by order of Governor Lord Dufferin (1826-1902) in 1879 to replace the existing postern gate. It was named for the Duke of Kent (fourth son of George III and Queen Victoria's father), general and commander-in-chief of British forces in British North America. It was rumoured that he fathered children with Bernardine Mongenet (known as Mme de Saint-Laurent) who was the Duke's companion in Halifax and Québec City, before he married Mary-Louisa, the mother of the future Queen Victoria, in 1818.

91. Chapelle des Jésuites (Jesuit Chapel)

At the corner of D'Auteuil and Dauphine streets, on your left, you can see one of the few traces of the presence of the Jesuits in the city. The Jesuits arrived in Québec in 1625 and established the first college in North America in 1635. But after the Conquest in 1759 the British Crown forbade them from recruiting and the college was closed. In 1800 the last Jesuit in Québec, Father Jean-Joseph Casot (1728-1800), died. In 1818 the Congregation of Notre-Dame de Québec began construction on the Chapel employing the plans of François Baillairgé (1759-1830). In 1849 the Jesuits returned to Québec; the Chapel and the adjacent residence have belonged to them since 1907. In 1930 two of their members, (1593-1649) and Issac Jogues (1607-1646), who had been martyred and killed in Huronia (the region of the Huron Confederacy), were canonized. Inside the Chapel near the altar there are statues of the two men by Alfred Laliberté. Since 1992 the Chapel and the residence have been a centre for homeless young people.

Information: 418.694.9616

92. L'Institut canadien (Canadian Institute)

Turn left onto Rue Dauphine to the Chaussée Écossais, a cobblestone pedestrian walkway. This is the heart of English and Protestant Québec. To the left of Rue Dauphine on Chaussée des Écossais is a church built in 1848 to the specifications of the Commissioners' Churches of England. (To receive funds from the Lords Commissioner of the Treasury the churches had to accommodate "the greatest number of persons at the smallest expense within the compass of an ordinary voice, one half of the number to be free seats for the poor.") Churches of this type do not have steeples because they were deemed to be too expensive to construct. The building was formerly the Wesley Methodist Church. The building was available because when the United Church of Canada was formed in 1925 two Protestant congregations, Chalmers United and Wesley Methodist independently joined the union, and then in 1931 the Methodist congregation left their church to join with Chalmers Church to form Chalmers-Wesley United Church. (Later, the Église Unie Saint-Pierre, a French congregation, also moved to the building.) In 1941 the city of Québec took ownership of the building, and during the 1940s it was transformed into a concert hall and municipal library that became the Institut canadien de Québec. (Note that it is not possible to visit the interior of the building.)

The painting by Luc Archambault on the wall of the square in front of the building near the stairway is called

"Nous sommes un people" (We are a people). It was completed in 2000 and commemorates the 150th anniversary of the Institut canadien. Just in front is the tiny Place de l'Institut canadien.

93. Saint Andrew's Presbyterian Church

Continue along Rue Dauphine to Rue Cook, named for one of the pastors at Saint Andrew's Presbyterian Church, the small church before you. This church is the oldest English-speaking congregation of Scottish origin in Canada. It began with soldiers mostly from the 78th Regiment of the Fraser Highlanders who had served in General Wolfe's army following the Conquest of Québec in 1759. The first pastor of the congregation was the chaplain of the regiment, Robert MacPherson. From 1763 onward, the congregation called itself the "Scotch Congregation" and served the civilian population. In 1802 a petition with 148 names was sent to King George III requesting that land be provided for the construction of a church; in 1809 construction began under the direction of John Bryson, and the church opened its doors on Saint Andrew's Day, November 30, 1810. The church's interior is in the style of Scottish churches, a rarity in Canada. Today there are about 50 congregants. If you visit, do not miss the gallery, called the Governor's Gallery in earlier times, facing the raised throne. You can also take a tour of the small museum adjoining the church which presents the history of the congregation. Guided tours are offered in July and August. Information: 418.694.1347

94. Jean-Baptiste de La Salle Building

Across from St. Andrew's Church is the enormous Jean-Baptiste de La Salle building. Abbott Jean-Baptiste de La Salle (canonized in 1900) founded the Frères des écoles chrétiennes (Christian Teaching Brothers) in Reims, France in 1680 to educate poor children. They arrived in Montreal in 1837 and then came to Québec in 1843. Today Québec's Ministry of Municipal Affairs occupies the building.

95. The Manse and Kirk Hall of St. Andrew's Church

Walk around the church on Cook and Ste-Anne streets and return to the Chaussée des Ecossais on your right. Behind the church are the Manse and Kirk Hall—the Manse (the pastor's residence) was built in 1836 and the Kirk Hall in 1829. The Kirk Hall was once a school, then the residence of the pastor (in 1885) before becoming an assembly hall and Sunday school.

96. Chaussée des Ecossais

Across from the Manse and Kirk Hall on the opposite side of the Chaussée des Ecossais is the Literary and Historical Society of Québec (44 Chaussée des Écossais), which was founded in 1824. The neo-classical building, designed by François Baillairgé, was constructed between 1808 and 1813 and was a prison until the prison was moved in 1867 to the Plains of Abraham (#118) to accommodate the prison reforms of John Howard. The building became Morrin College, the city's first English-language institute of education, from funds donated by prominent physician and former mayor Dr. Joseph Morrin (1794-1861). General arts degrees were offered through the College's affiliation with Montreal's McGill University. The College closed in 1902 but the present Morrin Centre functions as a cultural centre for Anglophone Quebecers.

In the middle of the Chaussée des Écossais there is an attractive monument to the Baillairgé family of artists, sculptors, and architects. Originally from Poitou, Jean (1726-1805) arrived in Québec in 1741; his son François (1759-1830), grandson Thomas (1791-1859), and Thomas's cousin

Charles (1826-1906) continued the line. The square you are in was created to honour the Anglophone community of Québec and their contribution to the city. Although Québec it is now an almost completely Francophone city (96 per cent), the English, Scots, and Irish strongly influenced its evolution and history.

The Morrin Centre welcomes visitors and offers guided tours. Go to: www.morrin.org.

97. Parc de l'Esplanade (Esplanade Park)

Return to Rue Ste-Anne (on your right) and walk towards Rue d'Auteuil—take a look at the charming Rue Ste-Ursule on your way—and turn left on Rue d'Auteuil to Parc de l'Esplanade. It was once a pasture, and became a parade ground for British troops in 1830. The park follows the fortress wall and is also the main departure point for calèche (horse and carriage) rides in the Old City.

Along the right side of the street there are busts of the great Italian poet Dante Alighieri (1265-1321), Russian writer Alexander Pushkin (1799-1887), the celebrated Québec poet Émile Nelligan (1879-1941), and Vietnamese poet Nguyen Trai (1380-1442).

98. Centre d'interprétation des Fortifications-de-Québec (Fortifications Interpretation Centre)

Continue along D'Auteuil to Rue St-Louis and the Interpretation Centre (100 St-Louis) located in one of the military buildings beside the St-Louis Gate. From the seventeenth to the nineteenth century there was ongoing work to enlarge and improve the fortifications by first the French and then the English regimes. The cliffs provide Québec with a natural defense on three sides, and this strategic advantage was exploited by the military. Together, all of the fortifications provided a complex defense system which had to adapt to the demands of the terrain: there is only one km between Cap Diamant (the Cidadel, #101) and Côte de la Potasse (Potash Hill, Artillery Park, #85), but there is a 73-metre (240-ft.) difference in elevation within that short distance. In 1693 the ramparts were constructed with pointed wooden posts and earthworks, but in 1712 the posts were replaced with stone works. Under the English Regime the defenses were improved—the Citadel was built and integrated into the fortifications. You can walk along the 4.6 km (almost 3-mile) fortifications and visit the gates. Remember that most of the ramparts were built by the British, little of the original French Regime fortifications remains. French-Canadians were not allowed to work on the improvements of the ramparts because, at the time, workers were required to have apprenticed in Great Britain to be allowed to work on the fortifications. Québec is the only fortified city in North America and has been named a World Heritage Site by UNESCO.

When you enter the Interpretation Centre you can visit the Esplanade Powder Magazine which was built in 1815. There were 15 powder magazines in Québec at the time that stored gunpowder in strategic locations around the city (#32). The Centre has been converted from its former military use to its current role as a museum, presenting 300 years of military history under three regimes. Not to be missed is the informative 90-minute guided tour "Québec—Fortified City". If it is raining, the models in the Centre are the next best thing.
Information: 417.648.7016 / Toll free: 1.888.773.8888
Reservations are required for the guided tours
Tour fee: Fee: Adults $10.00, seniors $7.50, youth $5.00, family/group $20.00

Interpretation Centre and Powder Magazine
Fee: Adults $5.00, seniors $3.50, youth $2.00, family/group $10.00

Hours: June 24 to September 4: daily 10:00 am to 5:00 pm. September 5 to June 23: Tuesday to Sunday 10:00am to 5:00pm

99. Porte Saint-Louis (St-Louis Gate)

The original St-Louis Gate was built in 1693 at the same time as the St-Jean Gate, and was also later demolished. The existing Gate was built by William H. Lynn for Lord Dufferin (1826-1902), and was inaugurated in 1878.

100. Québec Conferences Monument

Near the St-Louis Gate just inside the walls is a monument commemorating two historic meetings in Québec City, of Britain's Prime Minister Sir Winston Churchill, U. S. President Franklin Delano Roosevelt, and Canada's Prime Minister William Lyon Mackenzie King, at the height of World War II. The future Normandy Invasion was discussed at the August 17-24, 1943 conference, and the defeat of Japan and Germany's future was debated at the September 12-16, 1944 conference. The unveiling, in 1998, of the monument to the Québec conferences—bronze busts of Churchill and Roosevelt, with King missing—caused some controversy. As the CBC reported: "In protest, Prime Minister Chrétien even refused to attend the unveiling ceremony. But several historians maintained that King was only the host, so it wasn't necessary to include him."

End: St-Louis Gate

The narrowest stone façade house in North America with
the Price Building in the background. (#15 and 75)

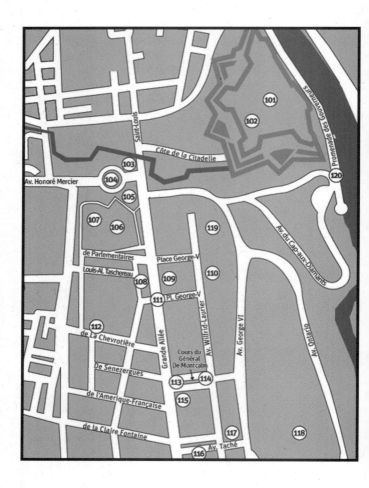

Av. Honoré Mercier

Saint-Louis

Côte de la Citadelle

Promenade des Gouverneurs

101
102
103
104
105
106
107
108
109
110
111
112
113
114
115
116
117
118
119
120

de Parlementaires

Place George-V

Louis-Al. Taschereau

Pl. George-V

de La Chevrotière

Grande Allée

De Senezergues

Cours du Général De Montcalm

Av. Willrid-Laurier

Av. George VI

Av. du Cap-aux-Diamants

Av. Ontario

de l'Amérique-Française

de la Claire Fontaine

Av. Taché

Tour 7

The Citadel, Parliament, and Battlefields Park

START: ST-LOUIS GATE

101. La Citadelle (The Citadel)

From Rue St-Louis take Côte de la Citadelle to the Citadel entrance. At the beginning of the nineteenth century tensions between England and the United States prompted the English to upgrade the colony's fortifications. In Québec City the building of the Citadel began in 1820 under the supervision of Colonel E. W. Dunford, and it took 30 years to complete its construction. The existing fortifications—the Old Powder Magazine (1750) and the Cap Diamant Redoubt (1693), the oldest military constructions in the city—were integrated into the new structure. The Citadel is a star-shaped Vauban fortification (named after the seventeenth-century French military engineer Sébastien de Prestre, Marquis of Vauban who developed this defense system), which is only accessible through the Dalhousie Gate. It is the most important British-built fortification in North America. Ironically, it was never needed or used for defense of the city. The Citadel is still an active military garrison. It is the ceremonial home of the Francophone Royal 22nd Regiment, and an official second residence of every Governor General of Canada since 1872. The Old Powder Magazine houses the museum of the Royal

22nd Regiment which contains artifacts connected to Québec and Canada's military history.

Guided tours are available daily. (Guided tours are necessary because this remains a functioning military base.) Parking is free, but access is complicated. Enter from Côte de la Citadelle.

Information: 417.694.2815

Changing of the guard: June 24 until the 1st Monday in September at 10:00 am daily

Fee: Adults $10.00, seniors $9.00, students $9.00, 17 and under $5.50

102. Governor General of Canada's Residence

At the Citadel you can visit the governor general's residence. The Queen is the Canadian head of state and the Governor General is her representative in Canada. Prior to 1867 governors of the colony resided in Québec City, but after Canadian Confederation (1867), Ottawa became the location of the official residence of governors general. In 1872, however, Lord Dufferin (1826-1902) re-established the tradition of a second residence in the Citadel of Québec.

Governors general have been present since the establishment of New France. Before 1759 they represented the King of France, and afterwards the British Crown. They hold similar responsibilities to those of a chief of state, and today occupy a position and function that is both symbolic (honouring and representing the Queen), as well as being commander-in-chief of the Canadian Armed Forces, and being responsible for the convocation, prorogation, and dissolution of the Canadian parliament. In 1943 and 1944 Governor General Athlone (1874-1957) received Churchill, Roosevelt, and Mackenzie King during the Québec Conferences (#100).

In 1872 the residence was a modest building dating from

1831, but there were numerous renovations and additions, including a ballroom and conservatory. A fire in 1976 damaged the eastern part of the residence, and repairs and restoration work was completed in 1984. The residence contains many historical artifacts, furnishings, and artworks by Canadian artists.

Information: 418.648.4322, 1.866.936.4422

Guided tours, 60 minutes in duration.

Hours: May and June: Sunday 10:00 am to 4:00 pm

June 24 to beginning of September: daily 11:00 am to 4:00 pm

September and October: Saturday and Sunday 10:00 am to 4:00 pm

Fee: Free

103. François-Xavier-Garneau Monument

After your visit to the Citadel return to Côte de la Citadelle and just before the St-Louis Gate take the passage under the Ramparts. Across the street is a small bust of Gandhi, and a monument to poet and historian François-Xavier-Garneau (#72) completed by Paul Chevré in 1912. The statue's bronze quill was recently stolen, so it appears that Garneau is writing on the wind.

104. Fontaine de Tourny (De Tourny Fountain)

Cross Avenue Honoré-Mercier towards the park across from the Hôtel du Parlement—the Parliament Buildings—and take a look at the de Tourny Fountain in the centre of the traffic circle, just recently installed to commemorate Québec's 400th anniversary. The restored fountain was a gift from La Maison Simons—a Québec department store chain founded by the Simons family in 1840. (There is a branch near City Hall, 78 Côte de la Fabrique.) The Tourny Fountain is one of six in existence worldwide, created in the nineteenth century by Alexandre Lambert Léonard and Mathurin Moreau and cast by the Maison Barbezat, a well-known foundry in Val-d'Osne in Osne-le-Val, France. The fountain's great beauty was appreciated in 1855 when, at the Paris Exposition, it won the gold medal. For more than a century (1857-1960) it was installed in Bordeaux (France), Québec's twinned city. The man symbolizes a great river, and the three women represent its tributaries.

105. Place de l'Assemblée-Nationale

The British troops used this site as their cricket field—and right beside the Fortifications was the building with a skating rink which was also used as a concert and exhibition hall. In 1879 the Québec government relocated the Parliament outside the city walls to this location. In 1998 the parkland was improved and numerous sculptures were added: the Honoré-Mercier monument (1912) by Paul Chevré honours the premier of Québec (1887-1891); a bit further along on the left is the monument to Sir Louis-Hippolyte Lafontaine, leader (1848-1851) of the first responsible government in the United Canadas. The Louis-Joseph Papineau (1786-1871) monument honours the leader of the Parti canadien and then the Parti patriote in the National Assembly of Lower Canada from 1815 to 1823 and then 1825 to 1838. In 1838 he took part in the Patriots' Revolt and was sentenced to hang—he saved himself by fleeing to the United States and then to France. He returned from exile when he was granted amnesty in 1844.

Continue walking through the park towards the right in front of the Parliament Building to the monument to Jean Lesage (1912-1980) created in 2000 by Annick Bourgeau. Lesage was premier from 1960 to 1966 during a period of great social change in Québec known as the Quiet Revolution. Robert Bourassa is honoured with a monument by Jules Lasalle. Bourassa was Premier from 1970 to 1976 and again from 1985 to 1994. The monument to René Lévesque (1922-1987) created by Fabien Pagé in 2001 pays tribute to the Parti Québécois premier of Québec from 1976 to 1985. Lévesque was in the forefront of Québec's independence movement. Right beside it is an *inuksuk* ("likeness of a person"), a traditional stone Inuit monument erected in 2002 as a symbol of friendship between the Inuit and the rest of Québec's people. It is constructed of stones from the four corners of Nunavik.

106. L'Hôtel du Parlement / Parliament Building

The Parliament Building was constructed in the Second Empire Style between 1877 and 1886 by Eugéne-Etienne Taché. It houses the Assemblée National du Québec (Québec's National Assembly). There are 125 members of the National Assembly (MNAs), which has been the seat of Québec's government since Confederation in 1867. The building's four 100-metre (328-ft.) long wings enclose an interior courtyard. There are 24 bronze statues of historical figures on the façade—founders, explorers, Amerindians, etc.—from before 1867. Since 1913 the government has added new ones: D'Iberville (1661-1706), La Vérendrye (1685-1749), De Sala-berry (1778-1829). A large fountain at the entrance pays homage to Amerindians with two statues by Louis-Philippe Hébert (1850-1917). *La halte dans la forêt* (The Forest Stop,1889), representing an Abenaki Amerindian family, was exhibited at the Paris Exposition of 1889. *Le Pêcheur à la nigogue* (Fisherman with Spear, 1891) is a sculpture of an Amerindian fishing with a pronged harpoon. Above the main entrance of the building is the coat of arms of Québec and . the motto, "Je me souviens" ("I remember"), that was officially adopted in 1929. It was Eugène-Étienne Taché who took the initiative to have it inscribed on the Parliament Buildings. This motto is an integral and implicit aspect of

Notre-Dame-des-Victoires Church (#53)

Québécois self-definition—"I remember my roots, my history." Québec's fleur-de-lys flag has flown above the Parliament Building since January 21, 1948 when it was adopted by the government of Premier Maurice Duplessis as the national flag (prior to this time it was the British Union Jack). The white cross on the flag symbolizes the Christian faith, and the lily the French roots of Québec.

You can visit the inside of the Parliament Buildings through the Visitors' Entrance (near Grande-Allée East, Door 3). There are guided tours available in English and French. You can eat in *Le Parlementaire*, the colonnaded Beaux-Arts-Style restaurant for the members of the National Assembly, which is open to the public.

Information: 418.641.2638, 1.866.DÉPUTÉS (337-8837)

Hours: Monday to Friday 9:00 am to 4:30 pm

June 24 to early September: Monday to Friday 9:00 am to 4:30 pm, Saturday and Sunday 10:00 am to 4:30 pm

Fee: Free

107. Pamphile-Le May and Honoré-Mercier buildings (and more on Place de l'Assemblée-Nationale)

Continue towards Boulevard René-Lévesque and pass the Pamphile-Le May Building to the left of the Parliament Buildings. Pamphile Le May (1837-1918) was a well known Québec writer, as well as being the first librarian of the Québec Parliament after Confederation. Built between 1910 and 1916, the building now houses the Library of the National Assembly. The Library, which was founded in 1802, had three major fires—in 1849, 1854, and 1883—and was moved to Ottawa in 1867 after Confederation. Nevertheless, the library now holds an important collection.

Beside the Pamphile-Le May Building is the Honoré-Mercier Building (constructed between 1922 and 1924 in the

Beaux-Arts style) which houses the offices of the Premier of Québec and the Cabinet Room. Along the length of the building by Boulevard René-Lévesque is the Premiers' Promenade. On the opposite side of the boulevard the large modern glass building is the Centre de Congrès (Convention Centre), which was opened in 1996 and includes a hotel and shopping complex.

Return across the small park and along the Parliament Buildings to Grande Allée Est. Across the street are two government office buildings, Complexes H and J (1967 and 1972), nicknamed the "radiator". In the park along the Parliament Building, there are monuments to Maurice Duplessis (done by Emile Brunet in 1960) and Adélard Godbout (by Michel Binette in 2000). Maurice Duplessis was the Premier of Québec from 1936 to 1939 and 1944 to 1959 (a record); his controversial reign has been called the Grande Noirceur (the Great Darkness), a time when many artists and intellectuals left Québec for France. One of his achievements was the bringing of electricity to rural Québec. Godbout was premier in 1936 and again from 1939 to 1944: women in Québec gained the vote under his government in 1940.

108. Parc de la Francophonie

Go past Rue des Parlementaires to the Parc de la Franco-phonie on the right, which commemorates the 25th anniversary of the founding of the agency that promotes cultural and technical exchanges among 50 French-speaking member countries.

A bit further along the building that looks something like a ski-boot is the Loews le Concorde hotel complex. At the top of the hotel is a rotating restaurant that provides a panoramic view of the city and the surrounding countryside.

109. Place George-V

On your left as you face Parc de la Francophonie is Place George-V, devoted to the military history of the city. On the square to your right is a monument dedicated to the Voltigeurs de Québec, a francophone light infantry militia which was founded in 1862. The monument was installed in 1990 facing a monument erected in 1989 in memory of the soldiers of the Royal 22nd Regiment who have died in wars and peace missions. Right beside it is the Short-Wallick monument, named for two soldiers, heroes who lost their lives while attempting to blow up a house in an attempt to prevent the spread of a major fire in the Saint-Sauveur Quarter of Lower Town on May 16, 1889. The monument by Louis-Philippe Hébert (1850-1917) was erected in their memory in 1891. The woman at the feet of the two men symbolizes the city of Québec, eternally grateful for their sacrifice.

110. Manège militaire (Armoury)

The ruins of the attractive building in the distance (805 Wilfrid-Laurier) was the Armoury or regimental barracks of the Voltigeurs light infantry. The Voltigeurs de Québec is the oldest French-speaking regiment (1862) in Canada. On April 4, 2008, a fire ravaged this landmark. The building was built on the fief of Louis Rouer de Villeray (1629-1700) and replaced an earlier wooden structure built in 1854. After the British troops left Québec following Canada's Confederation in 1867, the new country was equipped with seven stone armouries, including Québec's. The Armoury was built between 1884 and 1888 from the plans of architect and engineer, Eugene-Étienne Taché (who was also responsible for Québec's Parliament Building, home of the National Assembly). A large drill hall which was also used for ceremonies takes up most of the space and featured the largest suspended wooden ceiling in Canada. Most of the artifacts in the Voltigeurs Museum, one of the most extensive collections of military artifacts in Canada, were saved. These included items from the First and Second World wars, the Riel Rebellion, and uniforms and medals,

111. Grande Allée Est

Continue along Grande Allée Est (East). There are many hotels, restaurants, and cafés with welcoming terrasses along the "Champs-Elysées of Québec". The designation "Grande Allée" dates back to the French Regime when the street connected the Jesuit mission at Sillery (founded in 1637) with Old Québec. It has occasionally had other names—Chemin Saint-Michel road, Route de Sillery, Chemain Saint-Louis— but has returned to its original name. Until the middle of the nineteenth century the city's elite were concentrated in the Old City, but when Parliament was relocated outside the walls, there was something of an exodus towards the Grande Allée. Many of the grand buildings and residences along the Allée are from that time.

112. Observatoire de la Capitale

At Rue de de La Chevrotière turn right; as you cross St-Amable to your right is the Chapelle-du-Bon-Pasteur. The chapel was built by Charles Baillairgé (1826-1906) and, except for the façade which was built by François-Xavier Berlinguet (1830-1916) in 1909, inaugurated in 1868. As you come to 1037 de la Chevrotière, the building on your right is the Marie-Guyart Building named in honour of the founder of the Ursuline Monastery (#12). The Observatory is on the 31st floor, 221 metres (725 ft.) above sea level, with a panoramic 360-degree view. At the windows (you remain inside) there are information panels about what you can see from that particular angle. Don't miss it if you want an unforgettable view of the city and the St. Lawrence River. The sculpture near the entrance to the building, close to Boulevard René-Lévesque, is "1+1=1", created in 1996 by Québec artist Charles Daudelin.

Information: 418.644.9841

Hours: June 24 to Thanksgiving: daily 10:00 am to 5:00 pm. Thanksgiving to June 23: Tues. to Sun. 10:00 am to 5:00 pm

Evening access possible for groups by reservation

Fee: Adults $5.00, seniors and students $4.00, children under 12 free

113. Monument Montcalm

Return to Grande Allée, cross the street and turn right. Walk along Grande Allée past the Loews le Concorde hotel complex to the corner of Cours du Général-de Montcalm and the monument dedicated to Louis Joseph de Saint-Véran, Marquis de Montcalm (1712-1759). The sculpture, unveiled in 1911, is the work of sculptor Léopold Morice and architect Paul Chabert. It honours the French general who fought the British troops on the Plains of Abraham in 1759. He is seen here being crowned with laurels after being mortally wounded (#119).

114. Monument de Gaulle

At the other end of the Cours on Avenue Wilfrid-Laurier is the monument honouring former French president Charles de Gaulle (1890-1970). No one has forgotten his arrival at Québec on the cruiser *Colbert* in the summer of 1967 and his triumphal procession along the Chemin du Roy—or his provocative "Vive le Québec libre!" proclaimed from the balcony of Montreal's City Hall. The bronze sculpture, which was unveiled in 1997, is the work of Fabien Pagé. Return towards the Grande Allée and Montcalm's monument.

115. Nunavik House (Nunavik Information Centre)

Take a look at the stone *inuksuk* (#105) in front of Québec's Nunavik House (1204 Cours du Général-de Montcalm). The Centre provides information on all aspects of Inuit life found in Nunavik's 14 northern villages—art, food, and traditions. There is an exhibition of Inuit art and guided visits.

Information: 418.522.2224

Hours: July to September: daily 11:00 am to 1:00 pm and 2:00 pm to 7:00 pm

October to June: Monday to Friday 9:00 am to 12:00 noon, and 1:00 pm to 5:00 pm

116. Martello Towers

Continue along Grande Allée Est, and at number 425 you will find the residence of Louis-Alexandre Taschereau (1867-1952), premier of Québec from 1920 to 1936. At 388 Grande Allée Est is the former Franciscan Convent of Mary which is now an apartment building. At the corner of Taché and Wilfrid-Laurier avenues is the Martello Tower 2, one of four Martello Towers built between 1808 and 1812 by Governor James Henry Craig (1748-1812) to protect the city against a possible American invasion, although they never saw action. The towers, built by engineer Ralph Henry de Bruyères, were based on defense towers built in England in the early 1800s. There was a powder magazine on the lower level and a gun-carriage platform above for swiveling cannon. Tower 1 overhangs the cliff at the Plains of Abraham, and Tower 2 is on the other side of Battlefields Park before you. Tower 3 was demolished in 1905 to make way for a hospital expansion, but Tower 4, with the top floor removed in 1920, is at the corner of Lavigeur and Philippe-Dorval streets, a bit to the north. There are Mystery Theatre dinners in Martello 2— the guests must find the traitor in their midst—where you are served a typical nineteenth century English soldier's meal

in this unique space.
Information: 418.649.6157

117. Jardin Jeanne-d'Arc (Joan of Arc Garden)

As you pass quiet Avenue Wilfrid-Laurier, the charming small garden on your left is the Jeanne d'Arc garden, which was created by Louis Perron in 1938. There is an equestrian statue of Joan of Arc in the middle of the garden (also from 1938) which symbolizes the courage of the soldiers who fought on New France's soil during the war between France and England in 1759 and 1760. American sculptor Ann Hyatt Huntingdon (1876-1973) created the statue. Cross the garden.

118. Champs-de-Bataille Park (Plains of Abraham)

National Battlefields Park is more than 100 hectares (247 acres) of parkland created on March 17, 1908 by landscape architect Frederick G. Todd. Parc Jeanne-d'Arc, Parc des Braves, and the Plains of Abraham are all part of this immense park. Québec was attacked numerous times, but it was the confrontation on the Plains of Abraham that is the best known. In 1759 the decisive battle was fought between French troops under the command of the Marquis de Montcalm (1712-1759) and the English troops under General Wolfe (1727-1759). In 1759 New France was having difficulty in repulsing a fourth attack on Québec by the English who had been bombarding the city for the whole summer. On July 31 the French troops won a battle at Beauport, near Mont-morency Falls, but on the night of September 12-13, 4,000 English soldiers under Wolfe climbed the cliffs to Upper Town and defeated the French troops. Although the French had the same number of troops in the battle, the fighting lasted less than an hour because the French troops were disorganized. Montcalm was mortally wounded and died the following day, while Wolfe died the day of the battle. As a result of this battle Québec came under the control of the British until Canadian Confederation in 1867. Still today, the Governor General of Canada represents the British monarchy in Canada.

The Plains of Abraham are named for Abraham Martin, the man who owned of the Upper Town property around 1646, although he never lived on the land. This area of Upper Town has been called the Champs de Bataille since the Conquest.

The Champs de Bataille is a large park, but if you wish to do some walking you can visit the Grey Terrace, Wolfe's Wells, the Wolfe Monument and the Centenary Fountain. Or you can visit the Musée national des Beaux-arts du Québec, Québec's fine art museum.

Musée national des Beaux-Arts du Québec

The Musée national des Beaux-Arts du Québec opened in 1933 in its first building (to your right). In 1990 the building on your left, the former Québec Prison (1861-1971), was integrated into the complex with a Grand Hall joining the two together. The Museum holds a collection of more than 22,000 works, the most important collection of Québécois art from the colony's founding to the present day, as well as an impressive Jean-Paul Riopelle collection. There are both permanent and temporary exhibits.

Information: 418.643.2150, 1.866.220.2150

Hours: Daily 10:00 am to 6:00 pm, and from June to September on Wednesdays to 9:00 pm, closed Mondays from September to the end of May

Fee: Adults $15.00, seniors $12.00, students $7.00, children under 12 free

119. Plains of Abraham Interpretation Centre

Walk along Avenue George VI towards the Old Town. Just past what remains of the Armoury (which was destroyed by fire on April 4, 2008) is an entrance to the Interpretation Centre for the Plains of Abraham (835 Wilfrid Laurier)— with a tourist information office and a multi-media exhibit, "Odyssey: A Journey through History". It is an overview of the history of Québec, with an emphasis on the battle of 1759. You can combine the visit with others including the Martello 1 Tower and the Louis-S. St-Laurent House.

Information: 418.648.4071

Hours: Daily 10:00 am to 5:0 pm

Fee: Adults $8.00, students and seniors $7.00, children free

For the four activities: Adults: $10.00, students and seniors $8.00, children free

120. Promenade des Gouverneurs (Governors' Promenade)

Return along Avenue George VI towards the walls that encircle the Citadel. At Avenue Cap-Diamant (at the end of George VI) turn right and climb the hill along the fortifications to the belvedere which has an exceptional view of the park and the St. Lawrence River.

From the belvedere walk left towards the magnificent Promenade des Gouverneurs, the boardwalk which was built in 1960 around Cap Diamant under the Citadel. The view is spectacular. The Promenade's 310-step descent returns you to the Dufferin Terrace at the foot of the Château Frontenac— just in time for an *apéro* in the Bistro du Château ...

Monument to Monsignor François de Montmorency-Laval (#34)

Thematic Tours

Here are some tours based on specific themes—the list is not exhaustive, but the main attractions of each theme are included. During your tour, for descriptions of each place, refer to the numbers in this guide.

RELIGIOUS HERITAGE
1. Place d'Armes
2. Gérard-D.-Lévesque Building
9. Chalmers-Wesley United Church
10. Notre-Dame du Sacré-Coeur
12. Ursuline Monastery
13. Marie de l'Incarnation Monument
14. Ursuline Monastery and Marie-de-l'Incarnation Centre
17. Anglican Cathedral of the Holy Trinity
24. Monument to Monsignor Laval
25. Notre-Dame de Québec Basilica-Cathedral
26. François-de-Laval Interpretation Centre
27, 28, 29. Musée de l'Amerique français, Séminaire de Québec, Interior Courtyard of the Séminaire de Québec
34. Monument to Monsignor Laval
52. Rue des Pain-Bénits
53. Notre-Dame-des-Victoires Church
71. Bon Pasteur Museum
76. Hôtel de Ville
77. Hôtel de Ville Square

THE ENGLISH PRESENCE

101. The Citadel
102. Governor General of Canada's Residence
109. Place George-V
116. Martello Towers
118. Champs-de-Bataille Park (Plains of Abraham)

MILITARY HISTORY

1. Place d'Armes
3. Château Frontenac
7. Jardin des Gouverneurs (Governors' Gardens)
8. Parc Cavalier-du-Moulin
18. Museum of the Fort
31. The Ramparts
32. The Cannons
38. Prescott Footbridge
44. The Cannonball
51. Royal Battery
70. Maison Montcalm (Montcalm House)
85. Artillery Park
86. The Barracks
88. Saint-Jean Gate
90. Kent Gate
97. Esplanade Park
98. Québec Fortifications Interpretation Centre
99. Saint-Louis Gate
100. Québec Conferences Monument
101. The Citadel
109. Place George-V
110. The Armoury
113-114. Montcalm Monument, De Gaulle Monument
116. Martello Towers
118. Champs-de-Bataille Park (Plains of Abraham)
119. Plains of Abraham Interpretation Centre

ARTS AND HANDICRAFTS

11. Rue Saint-Louis
15. Monument to the Women Teachers of Québec
16. Artisans by the Cathedral
21. Rue du Trésor
34. Monument to Monsignor Laval
40. Casse-Cou Stairs
42. La Mailloche Glassworks and Economuseum
45. Félix-Leclerc Park
46. Jean-Paul-Godin Park (Traversiers Park)
49. Patrimoine Vivant Atelier
57. Place de Paris
59. Parc de la Cetière
64. Ex Machina
66. Place de la F.A.O.
72. François-Xavier-Garneau House
73. Livernois Square
74. Monument to the Teaching Brothers
87. Les Dames de Soie, Doll Ecomuseum
89. Place d'Youville
96. Chaussée des Ecossais
103. François-Xavier-Garneau Monument
104. De Tourny Fountain
107. Pamphile-Le May Building and Honoré-Mercier Building
112. De la Capitale Observatory
117. Jeanne d'Arc Garden
118. Champs-de-Bataille Park (Plains of Abraham)

THE WRITERS PROMENADE

A guided tour of Old Québec through the authors who have lived and or worked here. Two French-language and one English-language tour are available (May to November). Duration: 2 hours

Monument to writer François-Xavier-Garneau (#103)

Departure: Usually from the north end of Parc de l'Esplanade near the Kent Gate.

Information and reservations; 418.264.2772

Fee: $20.00

WHIMSICAL TOURS
La prophétie de Champlain
(The Prophecy of Champlain)

A treasure hunt through the street of Old Québec as you solve a plot based on Champlain's prophecy. "An adventure in which you are the hero in the streets of Old Québec." A map and a kit are provided.

Duration: about 2 hours

Daily, between 10:00 am and 8:00 pm, mid-June to end of October

Information and reservations: 418.687.6096

Fee: Adults $18.00, 13-17 years $12.00, 9-12 years $6.00, 8 years and under free

Ghost tours of Québec

A costumed guide relates stories of murders and ghosts as you are taken through the streets of Old Québec at night.

Duration: 90 minutes

Departure: May 1 to October 31, every evening at 8:30

Information and reservations: 418.692.9770

Fee: Adults $18.00, students and seniors $15.50, 10 years and under free

IMPORTANT DATES
(Celebration and festivals in Québec City)

January 1	New Year's Day
January 3	Bénédiction of the "petits pains" of Sainte-Geneviève at Notre-Dame-des-Victoires Church

Late January-early February   Québec Carnival
March-April   Good Friday and Easter Sunday
May 24   Journée nationale des Patriotes (Victoria Day
                     elsewhere in Canada)
June 24   Québec's Fête nationale
July 1   Canada Day
End of June to Mid-July: Québec's Summer Festival
Beginning of August: Fête de la Nouvelle France
First Monday in September: Labour Day
Second Monday in October: Canadian Thanksgiving
End October   Québec's Ghost Hunt
October 31   Hallowe'en
November 11   Remembrance Day
December 25   Christmas Day

Véhicule Press
www.vehiculepress.com